The Babes
in the Wood

A Pantomine

John Crocker

Lyrics and Music by
Eric Gilder

Samuel French–London
New York–Sydney–Toronto–Hollywood

ISBN 0 573 16409 6

Printed and bound in Great Britain
by Billing and Sons Limited
London and Worcester

PRODUCTION NOTE.

Pantomime, as we know it today, is a form of entertainment all on its own, derived from a number of different sources - the commedia dell'arte, (and all that that derived from), the ballet, the opera, the music hall and the realms of folk-lore and fairy tale. And elements of all of these are still to be found in it. This strange mixture has created a splendid topsy-turvy world where men are women, women are men, where the present is embraced within the past, where people are hit but not hurt, where authority is constantly flouted, where fun is poked at everything including pantomime itself at times, and, above all, where magic abounds and dreams invariably come true. In other words, it is - or should be - fun. Fun to do and fun to watch and the sense of enjoyment which can be conveyed by a cast is very important to the enjoyment of the audience.

Pantomime can be very simply staged if resources are limited. Basically a tab surround at the back, tab legs at the sides and a set of traverse tabs for the frontcloth scenes, together with the simplest of small cut-out pieces to suggest the various locales, (or even just placards with this information written on them), will suffice. Conversely, there is no limit to the extent to which more lavish facilities can be employed.

The directions I have given in the text adopt a middle course and are based on a permanent setting of a cyclorama skycloth at the back, a few feet in front of which is a rostrum about two feet high, running the width of the stage. About two thirds of the depth downstage is a false proscenium, immediately behind which are the lines for a set of traverse tabs. Below the false proscenium are arched entrances left and right, with possibly one foot reveals to the proscenium. A border will be necessary at some point between the false proscenium and the cyclorama to mask lighting battens and the top of the cyclorama. Lastly, there is a set of steps leading from the front of the stage into the auditorium, which I have referred to as the catwalk. I have imagined it to be set stage left, but it is unimportant whether it is left or right.

Into this permanent setting are placed various wings left and right, (I have catered for one a side set on a level with the border, but a greater depth of stage may require two a side for masking purposes). Cut-out ground rows set on the front or back of the rostrum complete the full sets. On smaller stages these cut-outs seen against the cyclorama give a better impression of depth than backcloths. The frontcloth fly lines come in behind the traverse tabs. Cloths can, of course, be tumbled or rolled if flying space is limited. It is a good tip always to bring in the traverse tabs when a cloth has to be lowered, then if any hitch occurs the lights can still come up and the actors get on with the scene. Similarly, I have indicated where the traverse tabs should be closed in frontcloth scenes so that there is plenty of time for the cloth to be flown before the end of the scene. The quick flow of one scene into the next is important if a smooth running production is to be achieved.

The settings and costumes should preferably be in clear bright colours to give a story book effect. Early mediaeval is obviously the best period to strive for in this pantomime, but, of course, deliberate anachronisms should be introduced into some settings and some of the comics' costumes. Animal skins can be hired from Theatre-Zoo, 21 Earlham Street, London WC2

Pantomime requires many props and often they will have to be home made. Instructions are given in the prop plot about any of the more awkward seeming ones. Props should also be colourfully painted and in pantomime most props should be much larger than reality. It is also wise for the property master to examine carefully the practical use to which a prop is to be put - it is very painful to be hit with a Giant's club of solid wood, one of material filled with foam plastic is far gentler!

I have not attempted to give a lighting plot as this entirely depends on the equipment available, but, generally speaking, most pantomime lighting needs to be full up, warm and bright. Pinks and ambers are probably best for this, but a circuit of blues in the cyclorama battens will help nightfall and dawn rising effects.

Follow spots are a great help for this kind of show, but not essential. But if they are available, it is often effective in romantic numbers to fade out the stage lighting and hold the principals in the follow spots, quickly fading up on the last few bars because this can help to increase the applause! They can also be used for the Fairy and Demon to give them greater freedom of movement than with fixed front of house or spot-bar spots.

Flash boxes, with the necessary colour and flash powders, can be obtained from the usual stage electrical suppliers.

The music has been specially composed so that it is easy for the less musically accomplished to master, but it is also scored in parts for the more ambitious. If an orchestra is available well and good, but a single piano will suffice. It is an advantage, however, if there can be a drummer as well. Not only because a rhythm accompaniment enhances the numbers, but also because for some reason never yet fully fathomed slapstick hits and falls are always twice as funny if they coincide with a well timed bonk on a drum, wood-block or whatever is found to make the noise best suited to the action. A drummer can also cope with the "Tings" noted in the directions though if necessary they can, of course, be done offstage on a triangle.

Pantomime demands a particular style of playing and production. The acting must be larger than life, but still sincere, with a good deal of sparkle and attack. Much of it must be projected directly at the audience, since one of pantomime's great advantages is that it deliberately breaks down the "fourth wall". The actors can literally and metaphorically shake hands with their audience who become almost another memb--- of the cast; indeed, their active participation from time to time is es-ntial. A word of warning, though, on this - the actors must always remair control; for instance, if a Demon or villain encourages hissing he must nake sure it is never to such an extent that he can no longer be heard. The roducer should see that the story line is clearly brought out and treated with respect. There is always room for local gags and topical quips in pantomime, but they should not be overdone. Most important of all, the comedy, as any comedy, must never appear to be conscious of its own funniness.

Characterisation should be very clear and definite. I prefer the traditional use of a man to play the Dame and a girl to play the Principal Boy. In the case of the Dame, anyway, there is a sound argument for this - audiences will laugh more readily at a man impersonating a woman involved in the mock cruelties of slapstick than at a real woman. For this reason an actor playing a Dame should never quite let us forget he is a man, while giving a sincere character performance of a woman; further, he can be as feminine as he likes, but never effeminate. The Nurse is sincerely devoted to her charges. Her manner is good-humoured and tolerant and reflects a boisterous enjoyment of life.

A Principal Boy also requires a character performance, but, of course, with the implications reversed! An occasional slap of the thigh is not sufficient. Robin should be thought of as a young man of great vitality, charm and determination.

Principal Girls can be a bore, but only if they are presented as mere pretty symbols of feminine sweetness. Maid Marion has a mind and a will of her own and is not afraid to use either.

The Babes revel wholeheartedly in whatever life offers. They are naturally mischievous at times, but not unbearably so. Sammy should seem a very typical boy with lots of guts and gusto and Susie a very feminine little girl with that well-developed maternal streak of little girls. This comes out most noticeably in her affection for Fred.

Wuffles, like the Nurse, is also devoted to the Babes. He is often baffled by the human standards to which he is asked to conform, which usually seem quite senseless to him, but he tries to oblige, nevertheless.

In outlook, Polly Flinders is essentially artless, the subtle approach is not for her, and though her intentions are always excellent, the results can sometimes be a little overwhelming. And behind all her strength is a very soft heart.

Muddles just muddles along, most of the time successfully.. His jaunty disposition enables him to bounce back again quickly after any little setbacks.

The Baron indulges in villainy as a way of life. He enjoys it for its own sake even though the results are seldom up to much.

The Demon has a more fanatical devotion to villainy. He is very devious in all his dealings, in contrast with the Fairy, who is very straightforward. They should be united in one thing - the relish with which they play out their struggle.

Herbert and Fred also have an interest in villainy, though they are very inexpert at it, as they are at most things except disaster. Their intentions are dishonest enough, it is achievement that is their stumbling block. Herbert blusters more than Fred but is really just as inefficient.

I have made provision for six members of the Chorus, but naturally the number used will depend on how many are available.

John Crocker.

CHARACTERS

BARON STONEYHEART DE STONEYBROKE	The Sheriff of Nottingham
MAID MARION	His ward
MUDDLES	His handyman
POLLY FLINDERS	
FAIRY NIGHTINGALE	
DEMON CATBANE	
SAMMY } SUSAN }	The Babes
WUFFLES	The Dog
NURSE JEMIMA BLOGGS	
ROBIN HOOD	
HORRIBLE HERBERT } FRIGHTFUL FRED }	The Robbers

SYNOPSIS OF SCENES

PART ONE

PART TWO

Running time: approximately two hours thirty-five minutes.

<u>MUSIC 1</u>. Overture.

PART ONE

Scene One - <u>THE VILLAGE OF MERRY-
DOWNDERRY</u>.

(Fullset. Cut-out ground-row of a village pond in the middle of a village green along back of rostrum. Steps down in C. of rostrum. House wing L. Wing R. as a forge with sign - "P. FLINDERS, BLACKSMITH" above a practical barn door the top half of which is set open.)

(CHORUS as VILLAGERS discovered singing and dancing Opening Chorus.)

<u>MUSIC 2</u>. "MERRYDOWNDERRY"

CHORUS: This is the village of Merrydownderry,
                   Where men are so handsome and girls are so very
                   Much ruddier than the proverbial cherry,
                       In this lovely part of Old England.

                   We are the villagers, neighbours adore us,
                   And even our enemies cannot ignore us;
                   There's no one against us and ev'ryone's for us,
                       In this lovely part of Old England.

(Dance)

                   This is the village of Merrydownderry
                   In Nottinghamshire in Old England.

BARON: (calling off L.) Muddles! Muddles!

1st CH: Look out! Here comes the Baron!

2nd CH: He'll try to make us give him all our money.

3rd CH: Quick! Hide!

(They run to hide behind wings. <u>MUSIC 3</u>. Enter BARON U. L. on rostrum)

BARON: (calling back off L.) Muddles! (turns) Has anyone here seen - ? That's funny, half the village was here just now. I wonder why that always happens when I come along? Well, I know how to get 'em back. (raising his voice and feeling in pocket as if to bring out a note) Anybody want a pound note?

CHORUS: (running on and crowding round him eagerly) Yes, please!

BARON: Ah, I thought that would re-populate the place. Of course, you all know what a pound note looks like?

CHORUS: Of course. (each produces a note and holds it out) Like this.

BARON: (bagging the lot) That's right.

CHORUS: Oh! Boo! Boo!

BARON: Now, now, none of that. I have my position as Sheriff of Nottingham to keep up and that takes money.

CHORUS: (gloomily) Yes - ours.

BARON: Well, my latest proclamation will give you a chance to earn some more. (brings out a scroll) Oyez! Oyez! Oyez! Ohno, Ohno, Ohno. This is me last week's laundry list. (throws scroll off and brings out another) This is it. Oyez, Oyez, Oyez - it is hereby proclaimed that the onetime Earl of Huntingdon, now known as the Outlaw, Robin Hood, is wanted for larceny, petty larceny, big larceny and medium-sized larceny. Any person delivering the said outlaw to the Sheriff of Nottingham will receive a reward of one hundred crowns. Signed Me, p.p. Richard Lionheart. There - and talking of money, that reminds me; there's an old friend of mine just gone on one of these Crusade things and he's appointed me his daughter's guardian.

4th CH: You mean Maid Marion.

BARON: That's right. Well, her father's asked me to find her a husband and as she'll get a very handsome dowry I don't want her falling in love with some village lad and wasting her lolly on him. I have - er - other plans for her. So while she's staying with me you will all refrain from talking to her.

CHORUS: Why should we? It's not fair. Etc.

BARON: Enough! I have spoked. Now I must put this proclamation up. Anybody happen to have a hammer and nail on them? No? How odd. I must find Muddles then. (going L.) But remember, no talking to Maid Marion. Muddles! Muddles! (exit L.)

5th CH: Well, that's not going to be easy, is it?

6th CH: No, we'll just have to try and avoid her. Come on.

(They start to move R.)

1st CH: Too late! Here she comes now.

(MUSIC 4. Enter MAID MARION U.R. on rostrum.)

MARION: Hullo, boys and girls.

2nd CH: Hullo, Maid -

OTHERS: Ssssh!

2nd CH: Oh no.

(CHORUS divide into groups and pretend to take no notice of MARION)

MARION: Oh no? How odd, everyone was friendly enough yesterday, now nobody seems to want to talk to me.

(CHORUS almost relent then intensify their efforts to ignore her. She sighs)

I shall talk to myself then. Lovely day, isn't it, Marion? Yes, lovely. Do you like it here, Marion? Well, it's a nice place, but the people are awfully snooty.

CHORUS: Oh, it's not fair, we're not snooty.

3rd CH: But the Baron said we mustn't talk to you.

4th CH: Because he said he didn't want you to fall in love with anybody in the village.

MARION: But that's my business, not his. Why shouldn't I fall in love with somebody if I want to? In fact, I will - I'll fall in love with the very next man I meet.

5th CH: But you don't know what he'll be like.

MARION: That might make it all the more exciting.

MUSIC 5.   "MY MAN"

    I'd like to fall completely for a truly handsome lad,
    And even plain good-looking wouldn't be so very bad.
    The fellow in my dreams was just as handsome as
                  can be -
    But I don't really mind as long as he loves me.

    The man with looks and nothing more
    Need never wait before my door,
    But if his love's a thing apart
    Then he has the key to my heart.

MARION & CHORUS: I'd/She'd like to fall, etc.

(Exit MARION R, with CHORUS. Enter BARON L, carrying proclamation)

BARON: Oi! you lot, come back here! You were talking to Maid Marion. Come back here! Oh, three naughty swear words, they've gone. Well, I'll deal with them later. I still haven't dealt with this. Where can that new man of mine be? Muddles! Muddles!

(Loud hooting off R.)

Ah, at last.

(MUSIC 6. Hooting continues as MUDDLES enters backwards R, holding a steering wheel to which is attached a bulb horn on which he is hooting. He bumps into BARON)

MUDDLES: Oops, sorry, Baron.

BARON: What do you think you're doing?

MUDDLES: Driving the right way the wrong way round.

BARON: Driving the right way the wrong way round. Why?

MUDDLES: 'Cos this is a one way street. (starts moving again)

BARON: Come back here. Where's my car? I told you to collect it from the garage where it was being repaired.

MUDDLES: I did. This is it. (offers steering wheel to BARON)

BARON: (taking it) What do you mean? There was lots more of it than this. There was all that nice bit in front and that lovely bit behind.

MUDDLES: I know. They took all those to pay for repairing them.

(BARON sighs and throws wheel off)

Oh, by the way, this letter came for you. (takes letter from pocket and gives it to BARON)

BARON: A letter? (opening it) Not another bill, I hope. (reads) Great heavens! Little Sydney! He's dead!

MUDDLES: Oh dear, I am sorry. Still, it's nice of him to write and let you know.

BARON: He didn't, you fool. This is from little Sydney's lawyer.

MUDDLES: Oh. Who is little Sydney then?

BARON: He was my brother. (greatly affected, leaning on MUDDLES' shoulder) My only brother.

MUDDLES: There, there.

BARON: And now he's gone. What a pity I never liked him, because now - (breaking down altogether) - I never will.

MUDDLES: There, there, there.

BARON: But at least his two poor orphan babes are coming to live with me.

MUDDLES: Oh, good.

BARON: Yes, it says so here - what! It does too. Two snivelling brats coming to live in my house.

(Throws down letter. MUDDLES picks it up)

Two more mouths to feed, two more backs to clothe. Where's the money coming from, eh?

MUDDLES: It says here they've inherited their father's fortune.

BARON: Eh? (snatches letter back) So they have! What splendid kiddiwinks! When are the rich little darlings coming to their loving nunky-wunky? (reads) Arriving with their Nurse on Wednesday.

MUDDLES: Wednesday?

BARON: Wednesday.

BOTH: Wednesday!

BARON: That's today! We'll never be ready in time. Muddles, go and get the spare room ready.

MUDDLES: (running L.) Right.

BARON: No.

(MUDDLES marks time)

I must meet them. Nip to the blacksmith and see if my horse is ready.

MUDDLES: (running R.) Right.

BARON: No!

(MUDDLES marks time)

I'm forgetting the proclamation. Nail it up somewhere. (gives it to MUDDLES)

MUDDLES: (stops, panting) Right.

BARON: Well, don't just stand there. Do something and hurry!

(Exit BARON L)

MUDDLES: Oh dear, he's got me so mixed up I don't know what I'm doing. Well, I'll see about the horse first. (he crosses R to forge, starts to knock, realises top half is open and kneels down to knock on bottom half of door) Mr. Blacksmith!

POLLY: (off R.) Oh, fiddlesticks!

(Large prop horseshoe sails over MUDDLES' head and lands with loud orchestra crash. He rises and picks it up)

MUDDLES: Hm, lucky.

POLLY: (off) And fiddledee!

(Large prop sledgehammer flies out of forge and lands at MUDDLES' feet, with louder orchestra crash)

MUDDLES: Hm, unlucky.

POLLY: (off) And likewise fiddle-faddle!

(Large prop anvil flies out and lands with still louder crash. MUDDLES backs L. MUSIC 7. Enter POLLY FLINDERS from forge. She wears a leather apron with pockets & carries a horseshoe in her upstage hand)

I'm fed up.

MUDDLES: So am I. Chucking things about like that. A bloke like you ought to be - eh? Coo, what a pretty blacksmith.

POLLY: But I don't like being a blacksmith. (kicks anvil) I never have liked being a blacksmith - (kicks anvil again) - And I never shall like being a blacksmith. (kicks anvil once more)

MUDDLES: Doesn't that hurt?

POLLY: No.

MUDDLES: Well, don't you be a blacksmith, then. (kicks anvil) OW! (clasps foot in pain)

POLLY: Just because my father didn't have a son to take over from him I don't see why I should have to. I'm no good at it, anyway. Look.

(She holds up horseshoe. It is square)

MUDDLES: Hm, very original. All you need is a square horse.

POLLY: Square horse! Pah! (snaps horseshoe in two and throws it off) All I need is a man to take over my job. Here, how about you?

MUDDLES: Me?   Oh no, I'm not a man - I mean, I'm not the right sort of man. Anyway, I've got a job. I'm Muddles, the Baron's new handyman.

POLLY: I'm Polly Flinders. Pleased to meet you. (shakes his hand vigorously)

MUDDLES: How do you - aah! (extricates hand, which is completely limp) Um. Funny, it's more flexible with the bones broken.

POLLY: I suppose you've called for the Baron's horse. Well, it's not ready.

MUDDLES: Ah, I expect it had the wrong shaped feet. Never mind, perhaps you could lend me a hammer and nail to put this notice up.

POLLY: Certainly. Here's a nail. (gives him large nail from apron) And here's the hammer. (picks up sledgehammer and passes it to him lightly)

MUDDLES: (drops it on his toe and dances round holding foot)   Ow!

POLLY: Shall I do it for you?

MUDDLES: No, I'll manage, but you hold these in place for me.

POLLY: Righto. (takes nail and proclamation and holds them against house wing L.)

(MUDDLES drags hammer over and tries to lift it. Eventually he manages to raise it a few inches from ground)

MUDDLES: (puffing) I - er - I think it's a bit high. Bring it down a bit.

(She lowers it)

A bit more.

(She does)

More still.

(She does. It is on ground level)

That's it. Hold it there.

POLLY: But nobody'll see it here. Look, I'll do it. You hold these up. (takes hammer and gives him proclamation and nail)

MUDDLES: All right. (miserably holds them against wing with outstretched arms and tight-shut eyes)

POLLY: It's difficult to see the nail, isn't it? (turns away and swings hammer)

MUDDLES: (opens eyes and moves head to look and covers nail with head) Is it?

(POLLY swings hammer and hits MUDDLES on head)

(turning) Well, I can see it all right. Oooh.

(He falls straight forward rigidly. The notice remains up. (Hole in wing to receive nail into which he has pushed it))

POLLY: Oh, Muddles, are you all right?

MUDDLES: (sits up rubbing head) Well - Ooh! I think you ought to find a job where you don't have hammers.

POLLY: I wish I could. I'm sick of hammers.

(She throws it off R. <u>EFFECT 1. Crash of falling metal</u>)

And of anvils.

(She throws anvil off. <u>EFFECT 2. Glass crash</u>)

MUDDLES: (rising) Careful. I say, I've had an idea. The Baron's ward, Maid Marion, has just come to stay with him. I'll see if I can get you taken on as her maid.

POLLY: Oh, Muddles, you darling! (hugs him)

MUDDLES: Ooh! Aah! Ooh! Could I just come up for a little air?

(POLLY releases him. He falls)

I said up, not down. (rises) I can see there's a few things I'll have to teach you if you're going to be a lady's maid.

POLLY: I can't think of a nicer teacher.

MUDDLES: And I can't think of a nicer pupil.

<u>MUSIC 8.</u> "A WONDERFUL LESSON".

POLLY: Teach me, teach me, teach me something new.

MUDDLES: One and one and one and one and one are two.

POLLY: How I wish that I were quite as smart as you,

BOTH: 'Cos that's a wonderful lesson.

POLLY: Teach me, teach me, teach me something more.

MUDDLES: Two and two and two and two and two are four.

POLLY: I always thought that school was such an awful bore.

BOTH: But that's a wonderful lesson.

POLLY: Love's a subject I would try;
I'd like to know the reasons why.

MUDDLES: But that's a most important i-
-tem you must never guess on.

POLLY: Teach me, teach me, teach me how to kiss.

MUDDLES: It's just a sort of kind of sort of thing like THIS!

(Kisses her)

POLLY: Now I know it, now I know it! Ah, what bliss!

BOTH: And that's a wonderful lesson.

(Dance)

POLLY: Love's a subject very new to me.

MUDDLES: Put your arms around me and then we'll see.

(They clinch)

POLLY: Now I'm sure of honours in my G.C.E.

BOTH: 'Cos that's a wonderful lesson!

(They exit L. BLACKOUT. WHITE SPOT UP R. MUSIC 9. Enter FAIRY NIGHTINGALE R.)

FAIRY: Good morrow, mortals. Nay, don't fear,
                        No harm shall come while I am here.
                        The Fairy Nightingale's my name
                        And I seek one of evil fame,
                        Who tries with never ceasing zest
                        My fairy pow'r from me to wrest.
                        But always with much sly pretence
                        That he has none save good intents.

(MUSIC 10. Looks off L.)

                        Lo! Here he comes. I'll hide a while
                        And mayhap learn his newest guile.

(She waves wand. WHITE SPOT OUT. BLUE SPOT UP L. DEMON CATBANE peers on D.L.)

DEMON: Ah! Is't safe? Aye, the coast is clear.
                        (creeps on stage stealthily)
                        That foolish fey my plans can't hear.
                        She doth o'er birds and fairies reign
                        And e'en to ruling me doth feign.
                        But I'll fullsoon expose this sham
                        For I the Demon Catbane am!
                        My scheme's a simple one indeed,
                        For those two babes who hither speed
                        She doth as Fairy Guardian fend.
                        But I their uncle's mind shall bend,
                        Till he their death shall bring about
                        And thus the Fairy's pow'r rout!

(He laughs fiendishly. FAIRY waves wand. WHITE SPOT UP)

FAIRY: Laugh not too soon. Thy scheme shall fail!

DEMON: (aside) Tarnation! Fairy Nightingale!
                        I must dissemble, soothe the sprite.
                        (to her) Methinks ye did not hear aright;
                        'Twas but a jest to pass the time.

FAIRY: Seek not to hide from me thy crime.
                        I warn ye, evil one, beware!
                        Harm not the babes by but one hair.

DEMON: (sighs) It grieves me much that you should still
Fear I would do the Babes some ill.
Why, I their lives do cherish so
My mind no other thoughts doth know.
(aside) That's true, at least. But 'tis their end
Not their survival I intend.

FAIRY: Thy true thoughts are but all too plain.
But deeds not thoughts will vict'ry gain.
So I will rouse up all my might
To guard the Babes against thy spite.

(Exit FAIRY R. WHITE SPOT OUT. DEMON bows mockingly after her.
FADE UP GENERAL LIGHTING TO HALF)

DEMON: Aye, do, it may afford some sport,
Though in the end 'twill win thee naught.
(looks off L.)
For here I sees the very man
I need to carry out my plan.
I'll step aside his thoughts to hear.

(DEMON moves upstage. Enter BARON L. studying letter and dabbing
eyes with handkerchief)

BARON: Oh dear, and yet again, oh dear.
Those two poor Babes make me heartsore -
'Cos they're so rich and I'm so poor.
Poor mites, how can they squander much
On toffees, ginger pop and such?
Perhaps the answer to the riddle
Would be to work a little fiddle;
In such a way that nothing's miss'd.
But how?

DEMON: I'll tell thee, hist! Hist! HIST!

BARON: (sniffing) I trust the gas pipe's not eroded.

(DEMON stamps and points to L. of floats. BLUE FLASH)

Ah, help! It is! The main's exploded!

DEMON: (moving down and bowing to BARON)
Your pardon, 'twas mere ectoplasm.

BARON: I see - it gave me quite a spasm.

DEMON: Well, rest assur'd, there's naught to fear.
I chanc'd your thoughts to overhear.

BARON: Oh dear, I trust they were not rude,
Sometimes my thoughts are rather crude.
I'd no idea they'd sprung a leak.

DEMON: 'Twas of the Babes that ye did speak.
I felt that I could help, perchance.

BARON: (holds out his hat)
                 Why, thank you, just a small advance -

DEMON: What? Oh, in bigger ways than that.

BARON: How nice. I'll get a bigger hat.

     (He starts to go. DEMON stops him)

DEMON: Nay, list. I would a scheme unfold
                 To win thee all thy charges' gold.

BARON: Splendid! But how? It's in a trust
                 So watertight it can't be bust.

DEMON: I think it can, one way I spy,
                 For just suppose they were to die -
                 What then?

BARON: The money comes to me,
                 Their only kin, but I don't see -
                 Oh, wait a minute, yes, I do!
                 But it's dishonest, naughty, too -
                 Oh, blow all that, I need the lolly.
                 Such sentiments are merely folly.

DEMON: Thou must not do the deed thyself.

BARON: No, no, I'd lose the lovely pelf
                 If I were charg'd with foul intent.
                 Besides, in some ways I'm a gent;
                 I must employ some underling.

DEMON: (producing a business card)
                 I thought perhaps -

BARON: (taking it)   The very thing!
                 (reading) "Horrible Herbert, Frightful Fred,
                        Enemies done for, friends cut dead."
                 I'll send for them without delay.
                 Ta ever so.

DEMON: (bowing) Farewell.

BARON: (raising hat) Good-day.

     (Exit BARON L. MUSIC 11. FADE LIGHTS TO BLUE SPOT)

DEMON: Full well he's play'd into my hand,
                 Soon naught my power shall withstand,
                 For, lo! unwitting of their doom,
                 The Babes come running to their tomb!

     (Laughs fiendishly and exits L. BLUE SPOT OUT, LIGHTS UP TO FULL.
     MUSIC 12. SAMMY runs on R, shortly followed by SUSAN)

SAMMY: Come on, Susan. I'm sure we're nearly there.

SUSAN: All right, I'm here, Sammy.

SAMMY: Where's Nurse?

BOTH: (calling to off R.) Nursie!

NURSE: (off R.) Coming children. Giddeup there, Wuffles!

WUFFLES: (off R.) Wuff-wuff!

(MUSIC 13. WUFFLES enters R., betwen a pair of shafts attached to a pram in which the NURSE is seated, holding some reins in one hand and in the other a stick with a bone dangling from it on a string in front of WUFFLES' nose)

NURSE: That's it, good dog. Right, whoa back, Wuffles.

(They stop in C.)

Here we are, all the way by dogcart. Help me out, Susie dear, and Sammy, you take this.

(She gives SAMMY stick and bone and SUSIE helps her as she puts a leg out and realises she is showing rather a lot of underwear)

Dear me, one is rather exposed here. Look the other way a minute, Sammy dear.

SAMMY: Righto.

(He puts stick over his shoulder so that the bone dangles behind him and moves L. WUFFLES sees bone and moves after it, pulling pram. NURSE tries to hop along on the leg she has got out)

NURSE: Oi! Come back! Stop! Help! Aah! (falls out of pram) Well, really! (sees that she is displaying even more underwear and hastily pulls skirt down) Ooh!

SAMMY: (running to help her up with SUSAN) Gosh, sorry, Nursie. Are you all right?

NURSE: (feeling behind tenderly as she rises) Yes, dear. It was just the blow to my pride that hurt.

WUFFLES: (straining round and eyeing bone longingly) Um-um-um.

SUSAN: Wuffles wants his bone.

NURSE: (taking stick and untying bone) Oh yes, poor old thing. Unharness him, dears, while I unharness his bone.

SUSAN & SAMMY: (moving to take WUFFLES out of shafts) Come on, Wuffles, out you come. Good boy. There you are, etc.

WUFFLES: (is delighted to be free. Thanks the BABES affectionately and runs over to NURSE jumping up and kissing her, dog-fashion)

NURSE: Yes, all right, Wuffles, nice kiss-kiss, but it's not helping me get it undone. This knot must be a great-granny. Ah, that's it. Now, Wuffles, what do you have to do?

(WUFFLES leaps up to take it)

No, no, you daft thing. You have to beh -

(WUFFLES looks mystified with head on one side)

NURSE: To beh - eh -

(WUFFLES looks more mystified and scratches head with forepaw)

To beh-eh-egg -

(WUFFLES looks totally mystified and shrugs)

To beg, you silly nut. Like this. (begs)

(WUFFLES - it all comes back to him. He begs)

That's it. You see - understands every word I say. (gives WUFFLES bone) Ooh, look at all these people. They must have turned out to welcome us to the village - isn't that nice? Let's introduce ourselves. (curtseying to AUDIENCE) How d'ye do? I'm Nurse Jemima Bloggs, and these are my charges, Susan -

(SUSAN curtseys. SAMMY takes out a catapult and examines it)

Very nice, dear. And Sammy - Sammy, put that catapult away - and Sammy -

(SAMMY puts catapult away and bows)

That's a good boy. And this is Wuffles, of course.

WUFFLES: (stands on hind paws and bows, holding the bone in his mouth and giving a rather muffled -) Wuff.

NURSE: That's right, only next time don't do it with your mouth full.

(WUFFLES returns to gnawing bone)

Now I wonder where your uncle lives.

SAMMY: Let's ask somebody.

SUSAN: If we can find somebody.

(They peer around)

NURSE: Not a local yokel in sight. (looking at ORCHESTRA) Perhaps those cave dwellers could help us. Seems a pity to disturb 'em, though. They look so peaceful fast asleep like that. Still, needs must when the devil takes the hindmost. (knocks on top of floats) Excuse me. (knocks louder) I say -

(All three knock)

ALL: Wakey, wakey!

NURSE: Dear me. It just proves there's none so deaf as sleeping dogs lying.

WUFFLES: Wuff!

NURSE: I knew you'd agree.

SAMMY: I know how to wake them. (whispers to NURSE)

NURSE: What? Oh no, I couldn't allow you to do that. Though, of course, if I happened to look the other way while you happened to do it, I wouldn't know anything about it, would I?

(She turns to SUSAN, while SAMMY gets out catapult and loads it with a paper pellet)

NURSE: Susie dear, have you seen that charming old village forge - (out of side of mouth to SAMMY) aim at the one in the middle - (to SUSIE) where the blacksmith works, you know.

(SAMMY releases catapult having aimed at CONDUCTOR, then hastily puts it away and looks very innocent)

CONDUCTOR: Ow!

NURSE: (sotto voce) Well done, my boy. (to CONDUCTOR) Ah, how fortunate you woke up at this moment. Could you direct us to the residence of the Baron Stoneyheart de Stoneybroke?

CONDUCTOR: No, we're only here to play music.

NURSE: To play music? Ah, the underground movement, of course. Well, Mr. - er -

(CONDUCTOR gives name)

NURSE: (repeats it) Ah, how nice. Do you think you could play us some music?

CONDUCTOR: Of course.

NURSE: Oh, good, it'll help to pass the time while we look for this house. You see, it's very awkward,we don't know what it's like.

MUSIC 14. "A ROOF TO HIS HEAD"

ALL: It might be a big house, a small house, a cot;
               It could be a bungalow, as like as not;
               It might be a barn, with some hay for a bed -
               But everybody's got to have a roof to his head!

BABES: It might be a pigsty where he's concealed,
               A nest in a tree or a hole in a field,
               It might be a castle, it might be a shed,
               But everybody's got to have a roof to his head.

NURSE: I've look'd in the fowl-house, the dog-house, the byre;
               I've crept into the crypt and I've climb'd up the spire.
               I've look'd to the north and the west and the south,
               And it feels as though I haven't got a roof to my mouth!

ALL: You've got to have a shelter from the day you begin,
               You've got to have a thing to stop the rain coming in;
               All the time that you're alive, and even when you're
                                                            dead -
               Everybody's got to have a roof to his head!

(They exit L at end of number with BABES in pram, NURSE in shafts and WUFFLES pushing. EFFECT 3. A horn is heard off R. CHORUS enter L & R)

6th CH: Did you hear that?

1st CH: Yes, perhaps it's one of Robin Hood's men.

(EFFECT 4. Horn sounds nearer)

2nd CH: No it's Robin Hood himself.

ALL: Hurray!

(MUSIC 15. ROBIN HOOD enters U.R., on rostrum and comes down to C)

ROBIN: Thank you, good people. A very pleasant welcome for an outlaw such as myself. And it shall be well repaid. (produces bag) Here is gold for the poor and needy of the village. (throws bag to one of CHORUS L)

CHORUS: Thank you, Robin.

ROBIN: (seeing proclamation) Ah, the good Sheriff has me in mind still, among all his other cares. I hear he has a ward to look after.

3rd CH: Yes, Maid Marion.

ROBIN: Maid Marion? I knew her when we were children. Tell me, is she pretty?

4th CH: Very pretty.

ROBIN: Then I'd like to meet her again. And if she's under the wing of the Sheriff of Nottingham I'd better stay on hand awhile lest she needs guarding from her guardian.

5th CH: If you stay here the Baron will catch you.

ROBIN: Why? I can always disguise myself.

(Enter POLLY R)

POLLY: Oh, blow - oh, bother and oh, I-won't-say-it-but-I'm-thinking-it! I've asked every man in the village to take over my job and none of them will. (to ROBIN) Wait a minute - what about you? You seem a fairly healthy looking specimen. (feels muscles in his arm) Hm, not bad; not as good as me, of course, but I daresay you'd toughen up.

ROBIN: I daresay I would, but why would I have to?

POLLY: Well, I'm the village blacksmith.

ROBIN: The blacksmith!

POLLY: Yes. Will you do it?

ROBIN: (laughing) All right, I will!

POLLY: (pumping his hand vigorously) Stout fellow! I can't thank you enough Mr. - er - what's your name?

ROBIN: Er - Hood. R. Hood. (extricates hand painfully)

POLLY: Mr. Hood. I'm Flinders. There's the forge, Mr. Hood, you can start as soon as you like. (bangs him on back) Cheeribye! (going off R) Muddles! Muddles!

ROBIN: (rubbing back) Ooh! Perhaps it's just as well she's giving up blacksmithing. Anyway, it's given me a perfect disguise.

6th CH: I think it's dangerous.

ROBIN: All the better. A little danger adds spice to life!

  MUSIC 16.   "THE SPICE OF LIFE"

                    Let me walk where the danger lies,
                    Where the lion lurks and the eagle flies,
                    Fighting hard for the things I prize –
                        That is the spice of life.

                    Let my friends be the roving kind,
                    With a steady hand and a thoughtful mind,
                    Never wanting to look behind –
                        That is the spice of life.
                    With my shield and my sword
                    I'm proud as a lord!
                    I would never exchange my role,
                    Never take the place of another soul.
                    Living free is the finest goal,
                        That is the spice of life.

                    I don't pick quarrels and I like good friends,
                        And I'd love if the chance came by;
                    But woe to a man if he offends!
                        Would anyone like to try?

                    Let me walk, etc.

(ROBIN exits R. into forge and CHORUS exit .variously. MUSIC 17.
EFFECT 5. Sound of approaching car. A cut-out car enters R. It
has a notice on the side saying: "DIRTY DEEDS UNLIMITED CO.
PROPS. HORRIBLE HERBERT, (WORMWOOD SCRUBS, PENTONVILLE),
& FRIGHTFUL FRED, (BORSTAL FAILED). ROBBERS OF THE FINEST
HOUSES IN ENGLAND". Car comes almost to C. & stops. Slowly
HORRIBLE HERBERT's head appears in front (HERBERT has a large black
moustache), and FRIGHTFUL FRED's behind him, both looking out front.)

BOTH: Hist!

(They turn their heads L. then R. FRED turns to his L. again and comes
nose to nose with HERBERT)

FRED: Aah! (disappears)

HERBERT: (yanks him up again) Ssh!

FRED: Sorry.

HERBERT: Hist! We're nearly there.

FRED: Ah!

(They disappear. Car moves forward again to L. and stops and the heads
come up as before)

HERBERT: Hist! We are there.

(Car suddenly reverses and stops C.)

FRED: Hist! We aren't there.

HERBERT: Well, this is near enough, let's get out.

(FRED disappears and as HERBERT gets out, car moves forward, flinging HERBERT on his face)

HERBERT: Oi! What's going on here?

(He rises and car stops L again)

Hey, Fred - where have you got to?

(Moves to back of car and peers over the back as the bonnet flap shoots up and FRED appears)

FRED: I'm here.

HERBERT: Well, get out of there.

(FRED disappears)

Ruin the engine, climbing all over it with his muddy boots.

(FRED crawls through car door)

Right, now we'll tell the Baron we've arrived, but first we must make sure we are unobserved. Let us reconnoitre.

FRED: Yes. (double-takes) Wreck a what?

HERBERT: A noitre.

FRED: A noitre? How do you wreck one of them?

HERBERT: It means we look round to see that there's nobody here.

FRED: Ah, but there is.

HERBERT: (startled, drawing out a pair of pistols) What? Where? Who?

FRED: Us.

HERBERT: I know we're here. I mean anyone besides us. Now keep close behind me and make yourself as inconspicuous as possible.

FRED: Righto.

(MUSIC 18. HERBERT circles stealthily round stage with FRED bent forward behind him hiding underneath HERBERT's cloak)

HERBERT: Right, all clear. Now we can call on the Baron, Fred.

(Turns to where he thinks FRED is beside him, but FRED moves round with him. HERBERT continues moving round until he faces front again, FRED moving with him)

Oi! Where are you?

FRED: (pushing face between HERBERT's legs) Here.

HERBERT: Get out of it!

(FRED comes through, his legs toppling him over)

HERBERT: Look out! Fool! Help me up.

(FRED bends to do so and is just pulling him up when BARON enters L just behind him)

BARON: Aha!

FRED: AAH!

(He leaps in the air letting HERBERT fall again and starts to run off R, but HERBERT grabs the end of his cloak so he has to double mark time on one spot)

BARON: What's the matter with you two?

HERBERT: Oh, nothing, nothing. (rises) Here, are you the Baron?

BARON: I am.

HERBERT: (moving to beside FRED) Hey, Fred, it's the Baron.

FRED: (turns, continuing to double mark time) The Baron?

HERBERT: (starting to double mark time) Yes, the Baron.

BARON: (moving beside HERBERT) That's right, the Baron. (starts to double mark time) Are you the men I sent for?

HERBERT: Yes, I'm Horrible Herbert.

BARON: (shaking hands with him) How do you do?

HERBERT: And this is Frightful Fred.

BARON: (shaking hands with FRED across HERBERT) Pleased to meet you.

HERBERT: No, no, the pleasure's ours.

FRED: Pleased to meet you. (suddenly notices that they are all double marking time and stops, looking at others in a puzzled way)

HERBERT: Well, now - (looks between FRED and BARON and notices that FRED has stopped) Oh. (also stops, rather self-consciously)

BARON: Excuse me.

BOTH: Yes?

BARON: What are we running for? (sees that they have stopped and stops himself) Oh. Yes, well, to business.

HERBERT: Certainly, to business. What can we do for you, Baron? We specialise in all types of crime, big and small, in the home or out of the home. See our testimonials from satisfied customers. If you have a crime that you want done then we're the firm for you.

BOTH: (with a little dance)
          Come to us, we're the firm to know,
          Dirty Deeds Unlimited Co!

HERBERT: End of commercial break. Now what had you in mind?

BARON: (after looking stealthily round) Murder!

HERBERT: Murder, ah yes.

(HERBERT and FRED draw daggers)

When would you like to be murdered?

BARON: Not me, you fool.

(They put daggers away, a little disappointed)

I want you to murder someone else - two someone elses.

HERBERT: Two? That might come a little expensive. What are murders running at now, Fred?

FRED: (producing a list and looking down it) Murders. Did you want them with killing or without?

BARON: With, of course.

FRED: With? Sixpence each.

BARON: Sixpence! Good heavens, don't you do any reduction for quantity?

HERBERT: Certainly. We'll let you have two for the price of two.

BARON: Done! (aside) A bargain, by jove. I'll give you the details. Listen carefully.

(FRED whips out a notebook and pencil. BARON looks stealthily round then whispers in HERBERT's ear. FRED waits, then sees that BARON is whispering and strains to hear. He cannot, so puts his ear to HERBERT's R. ear and starts writing industriously. As he does so his face gets sadder and sadder)

BARON: (straightening up) Right?

FRED: Yes. (bursts into tears)

HERBERT: (looking rather mystified between the two of them) Well, I didn't hear a thing.

FRED: (tearfully) You're lucky then. (gets louder with emotion each time) He wants us to take two dear little babes -

BARON: Ssh!

HERBERT: Yes.

FRED: Into the forest.

BARON: Ssh! Ssh!

HERBERT: Yes, yes.

FRED: And -

BARON: Ssh! Ssh! Ssh!

HERBERT: Yes, yes, yes!

FRED: Murder them!

(HERBERT bursts into tears on FRED's shoulder)

BARON: A fat lot of use you two are. I should think the whole village knows by now. Well, if you don't want to do it I'll take my money elsewhere.

BOTH: (completely recovering) Oh.

HERBERT: You've talked us into it.

BARON: Splendid.

HERBERT: We'll go and lay our plans. Come, Fred.

(They get into car. BARON moves to stand at rear end of car)

BARON: Good, but there must be the utmost secrecy and nothing must go wrong.

HERBERT: Leave it to us, Baron. Nothing we touch ever goes wrong.

(Car backs into BARON and knocks him over)

BOTH: Ooh.

(MUSIC 19. Car moves forwards and off L.)

BARON: (rising and dusting himself down) Tcha! Incompetent fools. Still, that's one fortune settled. Now I must win Maid Marion and diddle her out of her dowry. (looks off R) Aha! Now's me chance! Here comes me scrumptious little ward!

(Enter MAID MARION R.)

Greetings, my pretty dear.

MARION: Hullo, Baron, I've been looking for you. Muddles has found me a maid. I said you'd be very pleased to take her on.

BARON: (gulps) Of course, my dear. I'd do anything for you - anything. And can you not guess why?

MARION: No.

BARON: What? (clasping his R. side) Ah, can you not hear the passionate beating of my heart?

MARION: No, but if I could it would beat the other side.

BARON: Eh? Well, it's beating so passionately it's got all mixed up. (clasping L. side) It beats with love - for you.

(He moves to embrace her, she steps aside and he nearly topples over with his arms clasped round himself)

MARION: Oh no.

BARON: Oh yes! And I'll prove it as soon as I get me arms unstuck. (frees them) There. Come to me arms, me beauty! (chases her)

MARION: (running towards forge) Go away, go away! Don't touch me!

(She tries to duck under his arms but he catches her)

BARON: Aha! Now, say you'll be mine.

MARION: I won't say anything of the sort. Leave me alone!

(Enter ROBIN from forge, wearing leather apron)

ROBIN: What's going on here? Ah, the Sheriff. Here, stop that.

BARON: Oh, go away.

ROBIN: Go away - we'll soon see who's going away. Take that!
(hits BARON)

BARON: (staggering back) Ow! You great big bully. Knocking me
about. Just because I'm bigger than you are. How dare you clout my
Baronial lugholes, you beastly blacksmith. But you wait, you wait!
(turns and crashes into house wing L.) Oh, rude word upon rude word!
(stumps off L)

ROBIN: Did he hurt you?

MARION: No, I'm all right.

ROBIN: Good, but if that's how the Sheriff treats a lady I'm glad
I decided to stay here and safeguard his ward.

MARION: Safeguard Maid Marion? Why?

ROBIN: We knew each other a little as children. Also I hear she
is very lovely, but I'm sure she can't be half as lovely as you.

MARION: Well, we're both about the same, because, you see, I
am Maid Marion.

ROBIN: Then I'm sorry I didn't hit the Baron harder.

MARION: But who are you? I don't remember meeting a blacksmith
as a child. Still, I suppose you weren't a blacksmith then.

ROBIN: No, I've only just taken to the trade. When you knew me I
was Robin, Earl of Huntingdon, now I am -

MARION: Robin Hood!

ROBIN: (bowing) At your service.

MARION: But aren't you in danger here?

ROBIN: Why, yes, I think I am, in very grave danger, of falling in
love.

MUSIC 20. "DANGER OF LOVE"

ROBIN &   Help me! I'm in danger,
MARION: For to love I'm just a stranger,
                And it comes upon me swiftly,
                Like a shadow in the night.

Love comes like a bandit,
And I just can't understand it,
     For it sends its silver arrows
     From some ambush out of sight.

Love's deceitful, love's a liar,
     Love can sing most sweetly;
Suddenly I'm under fire
     And I am lost completely.

Your lips steal my senses,
And your eyes pierce my defences;
     So please help me, I'm in danger of love.

(Enter BARON L., followed by some CHORUS. Remainder of CHORUS enter R.)

BARON: There he is, that's the fellow! Now then, you lads, arrest him.

CHORUS: No, we won't.

(Enter MUDDLES R. with POLLY)

BARON: What? Ah, Muddles. Arrest that man.

MUDDLES: Eh? What? Me? My name's Muddles not Wyatt Earp. You're the Sheriff, why don't you arrest him?

BARON: Because I might get hurt, of course. But if it's authority you want I hereby appoint you Deputy Sheriff. (brings out a tin star and pins it on MUDDLES' chest)

MUDDLES: Ow! Mind where you're sticking that pin. Anyway, I don't want to be a Deputy. Polly would be much better. Let's make her Deputy. There. (pins star onto POLLY)

POLLY: What, and have to arrest my new blacksmith? Never! I know, we'll make him Deputy - he can't arrest himself. (pins star on ROBIN)

BARON: Oh, you are a rotten lot. Very well, I'll let the blacksmith off -

ALL: Hurray!

BARON: If he proves himself as a deputy and captures Robin Hood.

(CHORUS and MARION gasp. BARON takes down proclamation and thrusts it at ROBIN)

It's Nottingham Goose Fair in a couple of days. I'll give you till then to bring him to me.

ROBIN: And the reward, will you give me that too?

BARON: I suppose I'll have to.

ROBIN: Very well, Baron. On Goose Fair Day I promise I will - er - "bring" Robin Hood to you.

(Enter WUFFLES L.)

WUFFLES: (looks at assembled crowd and beckons off L.) Wuff!

BABES: (off L.) All right, Wuffles, we're coming.

(BABES enter L. supporting NURSE)

NURSE: Ooh, I hope we find the Baron's house soon. Me feet are killing me.

BARON: What's that? What do you want with the Baron? Begging, I suppose. Well, be off with you, you old hag, and take those beastly brats with you.

MUDDLES: Wait a minute, Baron, these must be the Babes.

BARON: Eh? Oh, of course, me lovely little rich relatives! Come to your loving Uncle's arms, my dears.

NURSE: I trust you're not including me in that offer.

BARON: Well, well, why not? A pretty young slip of a thing like you. (nudges her playfully in ribs)

NURSE: Ooh. It was old hag a minute ago.

MARION: Baron, don't you think we ought to celebrate their arrival?

BARON: Yes, I suppose it would look good. Very well, everybody, in honour of my nephew and niece I declare today a holiday.

ALL: Hurray!

MUSIC 21. "A HAPPY SONG"

> A happy song, a happy song,
> A song you'll want to sing the whole day long:
> You'll find tonight a cure for your sorrow,
> And you'll wake up singing tomorrow.
> You'll love the chime of it, the rhyme of it,
> Your toes will tingle to the time of it;
> You'll know that nothing in the world is wrong,
> If you sing a happy song!

BLACKOUT

Close traverse tabs. Fly in Scene 2
frontcloth, if used.

Scene Two. ON THE WAY TO SCHOOL

(Frontcloth - a village street - or tabs. If cloth is used, tabs to begin
opening as soon as ready during scene)

(MUSIC 22. HERBERT's head appears R)

HERBERT: Hist! (whispering) Fred, where are you?

(FRED's head appears L)

FRED: Coo-ee! I'm here.

HERBERT: Ssh! Well, you shouldn't be. Come over here.

FRED: All right. (disappears)

HERBERT: I said, come over here, not go away altogether. Oh, I'll
have to go and fetch him. Wait there - I'm coming over. (steps cautiously
onstage and elaborately tiptoes forward a few paces, stops, looks round
carefully, then belts across and off L. and looks on again) Made it. Now
then - Well, where are you?

FRED: (popping head on R) Over here!

HERBERT: But I just told you to wait for me over here.

FRED: Oh, did you? Sorry.

HERBERT: (turning head away, resigned) Never mind, wait for me
there. (looks back - FRED has disappeared. Moves onstage) I said, wait
for me there. Did you hear me? (stops) Ooh, I'm forgetting myself.
(runs back to L. and calls to R) Hi, Fred - Fred! He must have got lost.
I'll have to go and find him. (disappears)

(Slight pause)

FRED: (peering on R) I'm waiting. Herbert, I'm waiting. Well,
say something, Herbert. (running across to L) Herbert, where are you?
Don't leave me, Herbert. Herbert! (disappears L)

HERBERT: (entering R) Where has he got to? Hey, Fred! Fred!
Where are you? (exits L)

(FRED reappears a second later R., running to L., simultaneously with
HERBERT running on L., towards R. They pass each other calling one
another's names, then suddenly register, stop and run back, again passing
each other. FRED stops R. where he thought he saw HERBERT and
HERBERT stops L. where he thought he saw FRED. Both shake their heads,
scratch them in puzzlement, shrug and turn in)

FRED: Herbert!)
        (together)
HERBERT: Fred!   )

HERBERT: I do wish you'd stop mucking about. I take all sorts of
precautions to make sure nobody sees us and then you go and spoil everything by running around all over the place.

FRED: Well, you were running too.

HERBERT: I was not running. I was merely creeping quickly. Now
are you all ready for work? Have you got your sword?

FRED: (showing it) Yes.

HERBERT: Dagger?

FRED: (showing it) Yes.

HERBERT: Pistol?

FRED: No.

HERBERT: No? Why not?

FRED: I don't like pistols. They go off with a big bang and it
upsets my nerves. I've brought a pop-gun instead.

HERBERT: A pop-gun?

FRED: (taking it out of belt) Yes, it only goes off with a little pop.
You see you push this cork in the end here and then you press it and it goes -

(He pushes it and it pops into HERBERT's face)

HERBERT: Ow!

FRED: Did you hear it go pop?

HERBERT: Yes, I did and I'll make you go pop in a minute. For
goodness sake, let's get on with our work. What have we got on hand at
the moment?

FRED: (replaces pop-gun and brings out notebook) Oh, it's a
nasty job. I don't like it. Messy - Ugh - Kak-kah.

HERBERT: What are you talking about? What is it?

FRED: It's those murders for the Baron. I never did like murders.
They're bad for my nerves.

HERBERT: Well, we'll do it as nicely as we can. But first we must
think how we're going to nab the Babes.

FRED: (looking off L.) There's a couple of kids coming now. Won't
they do?

HERBERT: No, no, it must be the right - (looks off L.) Wait a minute -
it is them! What a bit of luck. We'll hide over here so they can't see us
then creep up on 'em.

(They crouch down at L. C. covering their faces with their cloaks)

FRED: How do you know they won't see us?

HERBERT: How can they? We can't see them.

(Enter BABES carrying school books)

SUSAN: Come on, Sammy, hurry up. We'll be late for school.

SAMMY: All right, but I don't much mind if we are. Coo, look.
(points to ROBBERS) Do you think they're asleep? Perhaps I ought to wake
them with my catapult.

FRED:	(lowering cloak) Don't you dare!
HERBERT:	(hastily pulling it up again) Ssh!
SUSAN:	Sammy, they heard you.
SAMMY:	Well, I was only going to do it if they were asleep. I mean, it's dangerous to go to sleep in the road. They might get run over or anything.

(They move slowly R.)

HERBERT:	(lowering cloak) Come on, Fred, now's our chance.

(FRED lowers his cloak and they creep after BABES on their knees)

SAMMY:	Oh, I couldn't have done it, anyway.
SUSAN:	Why not?
SAMMY:	Nurse confiscated my catapult yesterday.
HERBERT:	Now! (they start to rise)
NURSE:	(off L.) Hurry up, Wuffles.
HERBERT:	Not now.

(They subside to their knees and cover themselves again. Enter NURSE L with catapult, followed by WUFFLES who carries her books in his mouth)

NURSE:	You see how it works, Wuffles, you put a little pellet in here and then you let it go and - (lets it go and hits HERBERT)
HERBERT:	Ow!
NURSE:	Oh dear.

(She sees BABES. SAMMY folds his arms and looks at her quizzically. SUSAN puts a hand to her mouth to hide a smile. NURSE tries to hide catapult behind her back)

Yes, well, er -

(SAMMY leans out to look rather pointedly at catapult behind her back)

Ah, Sammy dear, I was just looking for you to give you back your catapult. (hands it to him)

SAMMY:	(takes it very innocently) Were you, Nurse?
NURSE:	Yes dear. Um. Are these two little friends of yours? (patting HERBERT's head) Dear little things. (raises HERBERT's hat) Are you coming to school, too?
HERBERT:	(in his gruffest voice) No.
NURSE:	(hastily replaces hat) Oh dear, nasty cold, poor little tot.

(WUFFLES puts books down and sniffs round ROBBERS and growls)

Now, now, don't frighten the little tinies, Wuffles. Come along, dears, off we go to school.

(Exit NURSE and BABES R. WUFFLES picks up books and starts after
them. ROBBERS lower cloaks as WUFFLES turns and gives them a
parting growl. They raise cloaks again. WUFFLES exits and they
cautiously let them down.)

FRED: I say.

HERBERT: Yes?

FRED: We didn't get them, did we?

HERBERT: No, but it's given me an idea. We will go to school. We
can nab them there. All we've got to do is disguise ourselves. Ah, Fred
me boy, in this business you need brains.

MUSIC 23. "YOU GOTTA HAVE BRAINS"

(Close traverse tabs slowly during number and fly out frontcloth)

BOTH: If you want to be a crook and thieve a lot of jewels,
               If you want to win a little packet on the pewels,
               You will not succeed if you're a lot of silly fewels -
               You gotta have brains!

HERBERT: The motto of our business is "Murder Without Tears".

FRED: It doesn't really cost as much as ev'rybody fears -
               It's ten per cent deposit -

HERBERT: And the rest in twenty years!

BOTH: You gotta have brains!

HERBERT: If you want a bloke removed without a lot of fuss,
               He happens to end up beneath a number seven bus,
               Or else beneath a number eight - it's all the same
                                                      to us -
               You gotta have brains!

FRED: If you know a chap that you want taken for a ride,
               We'll do it so that no one knows exactly how he
                                                      died;
               We dump him by a sewer and they'll call it
                                              sewerside!
               You gotta have drains - brains!

BOTH: Really classy doers-in and torturers are we;
               We bump lots of fellows off before we break for tea,
               We know how to do it, 'cos we always watch T.V. -
               You gotta have brains!

(They exit R. A schoolbell is heard being rung behind tabs. CHORUS,
dressed as schoolchildren and carrying slates and slate pencils, run
on L.)

MUSIC 24. "OFF TO SCHOOL"

CHORUS: We are the children of Merrydownderry,
               And we're on our way to the town seminary.

CHORUS: (continued)
>We are a collection of typical terri-
>-ble school kids of very Old England.
>
>Noses and knees in the pink of condition,
>We're off to the school to collect our tuition,
>And fight with the teacher a war of attrition,
>In this "conkered" part of Old England.

(Traverse tabs open to reveal Scene Three)

Scene Three. NURSE BLOGGS' ACADEMY

(Fullset. Cut-out of bookshelves with books along front of rostrum. Schoolroom wings L.& R. High desk U.R.C. with cane, chalk and duster on it and papers under desk-flap. Blackboard on easel U.L.C. Two benches running diagonally L. and two running diagonally R.)

(NURSE is discovered C. in cap and gown, ringing bell vigorously. BABES run on R. with slates and slate pencils to join CHORUS and all chatter excitedly)

NURSE: Schooltime, children. Quietly, please. Quietly! There's too much noise.

(They are silent)

Who's making all the noise?

ALL: Please, teacher, you are.

NURSE: What? (realises she is still ringing bell and stops) Oh. (places it under desk) Silly me. Right, you may sit down.

(They rush to the benches and seat themselves, CHORUS on the rear benches L.& R, SUSAN and SAMMY on upstage end of front L. bench)

I'm very glad you're all here on time this morning; if there is one thing I will not up with put, it's lateness.

(BARON in a Little Lord Fauntleroy suit, POLLY in a gymslip several sizes too small and MUDDLES in a schoolboy's cap, a very tight blazer and very short shorts run on R. All carry slates and slate pencils. NURSE looks at them wonderingly)

ALL THREE: Are we late?

NURSE: By about twenty years, I should think. What are you three doing here? I thought you owned the school, Baron.

BARON: I do, but I can't diddle the Min of Ed out of a grant if there aren't enough pupils so we've come to make up the numbers.

NURSE: Then as seniors you should set a better example of punctuality. You must all bend over.

(They do. NURSE picks up cane)

BARON: Why, is it time for gym?

NURSE: (pulling sleeve back) No, vim! (gives them a whack each)

BARON: Ow! (straightens up rubbing behind)

POLLY: Ow! (straightens up rubbing behind)

MUDDLES: Ow! (straightens up rubbing behind) I knew we'd suffer
in the end.

NURSE: Now you may sit down.

POLLY: (ruefully) I'm not sure I want to.

(BARON and POLLY sit on front bench L. MUDDLES is pushed off the downstage end)

NURSE: Now, now, Muddles, no playing about in class.

MUDDLES: I wasn't playing about.

NURSE: Ah, ah - don't argue with teacher, Muddles. Just sit down properly, dear.

(MUDDLES, mumbling to himself, pushes himself onto downstage end of bench and SAMMY gets pushed off upstage end)

Sammy, there's no need to copy Muddles. If anybody does that again I shall have to deal with them. Sit down, Sammy.

(SAMMY pushes himself onto bench and MUDDLES is pushed off other end. BARON takes out a newspaper and begins to read it. NURSE picks up cane and beckons with a finger)

Muddles.

MUDDLES: (rising) No, it's not fair, I didn't do anything.

NURSE: Come along, Muddles.

MUDDLES: (crossing to her) But I was just sitting there, minding my own business -

NURSE: Naughty, Muddles. Bend over.

MUDDLES: (doing so) Minding my own business, when suddenly -

(She whacks him)

Ow!

NURSE: Now, you won't do that again, will you, Muddles?

MUDDLES: (rubbing behind) Not if you're going to do that again.

NURSE: You'd better sit over there where you won't get into trouble.

MUDDLES: (moving to downstage end of front R. bench) All right, but I promise it won't happen again. (sits on very end of bench so it tips up and he lands on floor) Couldn't I just sit on the floor?

(NURSE shakes head and beckons)

1st CH: (on downstage end of rear R. bench, handing him a book and whispering) Here, take this.

MUDDLES: What for? I shan't have time to read anything.

1st CH: Put it in your trousers, then it won't hurt.

MUDDLES: (puts book in front of trousers and crosses to NURSE) Hm, seems silly to me.

(He bends over. NURSE whacks him)

Ow! (returns and hands back book) Thanks, but it hurt just as much. (nearly sits on end of bench again then firmly plants himself in the middle)

NURSE: Now, for the first lesson today -

BARON: (looking up from paper) Anyone know what won the 2.30
        yesterday?

NURSE: I beg your pardon?

BARON: Anyone know what won the 2.30 yesterday?

NURSE: Baron, come out here at once.

(BARON rises and crosses to her)

Encouraging these young things to gamble. You ought to be ashamed of
yourself. Bend over.

(He does so. She whacks him)

BARON: Ow!

NURSE: Now go and sit with Muddles.

(BARON sits Upstage of MUDDLES, and goes to sleep)

Does anyone know what won the 2.30 indeed.

2nd CH: (holding up hand) Please, teacher, I do.

NURSE: Oh, really, dear, what? I mean - er - hm - see me in the
        break, dear. Now, as I was saying -

(POLLY is looking at something on seat beside her. She wriggles away
from it slightly, holding up her hand)

POLLY: Please, teacher.

NURSE: Later, dear. For the first lesson we'll take -

(HERBERT and FRED poke their heads on R)

BOTH: Hist!

NURSE: -tory. Eh?

(She looks round as they come creeping in disguised as little girls. Both
have retained their belts with their arsenal of weapons, and carry slates
and slate pencils)

Good gracious! Hey, just a minute. You needn't think that by creeping in
you'll get away with it. I'm afraid you'll have to bend over.

(They are mystified by this, but comply. She gives them a whack each)

HERBERT: Ow!

FRED: Ow!

HERBERT: What was that for?

NURSE: Because you're late of course.

HERBERT: We're not late. We've only just decided to come to school.

NURSE: Oh, I'm so sorry. In that case, I take it all back.

(She hands them the cane over her arm as if presenting a sword then obligingly bends over and they give her a whack each)

NURSE: Oo! OO!

(They present cane back to her)

Thank you.

BOTH: No, no, thank you.

NURSE: What are your names?

HERBERT: Er - I'm - (puts on a piping voice) I'm Herbertina.
(curtseys) And this is Frederica. (aside, nudging FRED) Go on, Fred.

(FRED curtseys clumsily).

NURSE: I see. Tell me, Herbertina, have you always had that five o'clock shadow?

HERBERT: (puts up hand and feels moustache. Clicks fingers in disgust) Oh, yes - er - you see, my mother was a bearded lady.

NURSE: Really? What a coincidence. My father was a bearded man.

POLLY: (looking at seat beside her and wriggling and holding up hand) Please, teacher.

NURSE: Later, dear. You two had better let me have those toys.
(points to ROBBERS' armoury)

HERBERT: Toys? These aren't toys, they're real.

NURSE: Are they? Tut, the things they give away with cornflakes nowadays. Well, they'll definitely have to be confiscated.

HERBERT: You can't take these. We need -

NURSE: (tapping on desk with cane) Hand them over.

HERBERT: Oh, all right.

(He gives her his weapons. FRED undoes his belt to do likewise and his skirt comes down showing his shirt-tails without his realising)

Oi! (points frantically at shirt-tails)

FRED: Eh?

NURSE: Your - er - slip is showing, Frederica.

FRED: I haven't got a - (looks down) Ooh! (hurriedly pulls skirt on again, but has trouble with it) It won't stay up.

(NURSE gives him back belt)

Ah.

NURSE: You may sit down now, dears.

(They move to front bench R.)

```
POLLY:    (holding up hand)      )           (HERB:  Well, give us some room,
          Oh, please, teacher! ) together (       then.
                                )           (
NURSE:    I've said later, Polly,)          (FRED:  Shift up.
          dear.                 )           (
                                )           (MUDDLES:  Mind out!
```

(MUDDLES lands on floor again as NURSE turns back from POLLY)

MUDDLES: No, it wasn't me, it was them, they pushed.

NURSE: Come along, Muddles.

(MUDDLES rises and shrugs resigned, crosses to her and bends over.
As he does so he notices his shoelace is undone and bends a little
further to do it up just as NURSE moves can to whack him and it
sails over his head)

MUDDLES: (straightening up) That's funny. I didn't feel it that time.
(returns to his place)

NURSE: (looking at cane, puzzled) There must be a hole in this
can. (puts it down) Now then, history.

POLLY: (holding up hand and bouncing up and down) Oh, please,
please, teacher!

NURSE: Really, Polly. Can't it wait?

POLLY: No, it can't. There's a spider here.

NURSE: Oh, is that all.

POLLY: I'm terrified of spiders.

NURSE: (moves down and whisks it away with sleeve of gown)
There, it's gone now. It was only a little money spider.

BARON: (waking with a start) Money, where?

NURSE: Nowhere, go back to sleep. I man, pay attention to the
history lesson. Now a spider reminds us -

BARON: (looking closely at HERBERT & FRED) I say, haven't
I seen you two before somewhere?

ROBBERS: Ssh!

NURSE: Quiet over there. A spider -

BARON: No, bit I'm sure I have.

HERBERT: Ssh! We're after the babes in disguise.

BARON: But the babes aren't in disguise.

HERBERT: No, we're in disguise.

NURSE: Quiet, please. A spider -

BARON: What? Oh yes, I see now.

NURSE: Really, I cannot have all this whispering.

BARON &
ROBBERS: Sorry, teacher.

NURSE: I should think so, too.   Where was I? Oh yes, history
and the spider. Well, that, of course, reminds us of the famous story
of Robert the Muffet and little Miss Bruce. She, you'll remember, went
to make herself a junket and left Robert the Muffet to look after a cake,
or bannock as they say in Scotland, but he became so interested in
a rather trying spider that he burnt the bannock. Whereupon, she
clipped him over the lughole with a handy tuffet and that's how the battle
of Bannockburn started. The date, of course, was 1066. (writes 1066
on blackboard)

POLLY: Please, teacher, I don't think that's right.

NURSE: Not right? Not right! Of course it's right. I was there.
I remember it all distinctly.

POLLY: You were there in 1066?

NURSE: I can see you're going to be awkward. You'd better go
and sit over there with the other naughty ones.

(POLLY crosses to R.bench)

We'll move on. Where's the chalk? (she searches over top of desk,
then inside it, flinging papers out wholesale)

HERBERT: (aside to FRED) Come on, now's our chance to get near
the Babes.

(ROBBERS cross on all fours to L.bench and sit hurriedly as NURSE
looks up and notices she is holding chalk in L.hand)

NURSE: Silly me, had it in me hand all the time. (turning to R)
Now, Herbertina - (is disconcerted not to see him and swivels head
round and takes on ROBBERS L) Playing musical chairs, or something? (throwing him duster) Clean the board, Herbertina, and let
us return to our muttons.

(HERBERT cleans board. MUDDLES rises)

MUDDLES: Oh, good, is it lunch time?

NURSE: No, no, a mere figure of speech, Muddles.

MUDDLES: (sitting) A figure? That's arithmetic, isn't it?

NURSE: Exactly. Hands up any child who can tell me how many
beans make five.

POLLY: (putting hand up) Five.

MUDDLES: (putting hand up) Four.

SAMMY: (putting hand up) Three.

SUSAN: (putting hand up) Two.

FRED: (putting hand up) One.

NURSE: (banging cane down on desk) Sold to the lady there. I
beg your pardon. (goes to board and writes each figure down as she
says them) Well, one of you said five, one of you said four, one three,
one two and one of you said one. (draws a line under column of figures)
And that comes to - let me see -

POLLY: Fifteen.

NURSE: (rather taken aback) Does it? One and two are - er -
yes and three's four and four is, well, tice four are nine, of course,
and five makes - (counting on fingers) - um - thirteen. (writes 13)
Which is the correct answer. Thirteen beans make five. Now,
Poetry. Any of you know any recitations?

SUSAN: Yes, I know one.

NURSE: Oh, good girl, Susie. What's it called?

SUSAN: (rises) Napoleon's farewell to his army.

NURSE: Very nice, too. Give her a little encouragement,
dears. (leads a polite round of applause)

SUSAN: (bows and clears her throat) "Napoleon's Farewell To
His Army". (looks very serious and places her fingers to represent
Napoleon with his fingers in his waistcoat) Adieu. (bows and sits down)

NURSE: (looks at her and speaks after a pause) Yes. Well
thank you, Susie. Now, as it's the first day of term I want you all
to write to your parents telling them how happy you are to be back at
school.

(Groan from class)

Now, now, not too much enthusiasm please. All take your slates and
write what I say.

ALL: (writing on slates) What I say. (they hold them up)

NURSE: No, no, no. I want you to write a letter.

MUDDLES: Which one? There are twenty-six of 'em, you know.

NURSE: Don't you understand? I want to dictate.

BARON: (rising) You want to dictate?

POLLY: (rising) To dictate here in England?

MUDDLES: (rising) The home of the free?

ROBBERS: (rising) Shame on you!

ALL FIVE: We'll have no dictators here!

(MUDDLES produces small Union Jack)

ALL FIVE: (singing)
Land of Hope and Glory,
Mother of the Free -

NURSE: Shurrup! I don't mean that kind of dictating. I mean -
oh, never mind. If you want to sing we will sing. It just so happens I

NURSE: (continuted) have a song here all about one of our pupils - Little Polly Flinders.

POLLY: About me?

NURSE: Yes, dear, and as it's about you, you can give out the music.

(Gives music sheets to POLLY which she distributes)

(to CONDUCTOR) Are you awake .... dear?

(SAMMY gets catapult out)

CONDUCTOR: Yes.

NURSE: That's a good boy. No, we shan't need it this time, Sammy. (handing CONDUCTOR a sheet of music) We'd like a drop of this, please. (she leads and conducts number with cane)

MUSIC 25. "LITTLE POLLY FLINDERS" (set in the manner of Mozart)

ALL: Little Polly, Polly Flinders,
      Sat among the cinders,
      Little Polly, Polly Flinders,
      Sat among the cinders, the cinders,
      Warming her pretty little toes.
        Her pretty little toes.

      Her mother came and caught her,
      And whipp'd her little daughter
      For spoiling her nice new clothes,
      Her nice new clothes.
      Her mother came and caught her,
      And whipp'd her little daughter
      For spoiling her nice new clothes,
      Her nice new clothes.

      Little Polly, Polly Flinders,
      She sat among the cinders,
        The cinders.

BLACKOUT

(Close traverse tabs. Fly in Scene Four frontcloth, if used)

Scene Four. ON THE WAY HOME

(Frontcloth or tabs. (Scene Two cloth could be used again.) If cloth is used, tabs to begin)

(MUSIC 26. Enter WUFFLES L.)

(WUFFLES trots to C., looks off R., cannot see anybody coming, shrugs and sits on haunches facing Audience. He yawns hugely, remembers his manners and puts a paw to his mouth, then uses it to scratch his chest idly, the R.side of his face and over the top of his head to scratch the other side. He puts his paw down and sees his tail which he eyes suspiciously) Wuff! (He makes a grab for it, misses, chases it in a circle one way, loses sight of it, stops, sees it again and chases it in a circle the other way, loses sight of it again, stops, looks between legs for it, tries to get at it and turns a somersault. He kicks his legs in the air, gets on his feet again, shakes himself, sees tail again, grabs at it and gets it. He is very pleased with himself, takes a large bite at it and immediately releases it with a loud "yelp", jumping into the air and landing on his tummy. He picks himself up forlornly)

(Music ends. Open traverse tabs to reveal cloth if used. Enter BABES R. WUFFLES jumps up and greets them effusively)

BABES: Hullo, Wuffles.

SUSAN: Have you come to see us home from school?

(WUFFLES nods)

SUSAN: How nice. He thinks we need looking after, Sammy.

(WUFFLES nods and sets out to L.)

SAMMY: We can't run into much trouble between here and home, Wuffles.

(MUSIC 27. ROBBERS heads appear R.)

ROBBERS: Hist!

(SUSAN jumps a little and they stop)

SUSAN: Oh, what's that?

(ROBBERS creep onstage and smile ingratiatingly)

SAMMY: It's only Herbertina and Frederica.

WUFFLES: Grr-grr.

SAMMY: All right, Wuffles. Hullo, you two.

HERBERT: (aside to FRED. Nudging him) Go on, do your stuff, like I told you.

FRED: Er - hullo - er - my mum wondered if you'd like to come to tea with us my mum did, didn't my mum?

HERBERT: Yes, your mum did. And it's a lovely spread your mum's got, isn't it? (nudges FRED)

FRED: Oh yes, my mum's very fat, my mum is.

HERBERT: No, no, the food - tell 'em about the food.

FRED: Oh, well, there's beer and fish and chips and cheese and
pickles and -

SAMMY: I say, that sounds much nicer than the kind of teas Nurse
gives us, doesn't it, Susie?

SUSAN: Well, I'm not sure. But anyway, it's supper time now.
We ought to be getting home.

HERBERT: Oh. In that case, I think we'll have to persuade 'em to
come to tea, won't we, Fred - erica? (closes in to R,of BABES)

FRED: (moving to their L) Yes, I suppose we will, Herbert - ina.

ROBBERS: Come along, now.

(WUFFLES has been eyeing ROBBERS disapprovingly and now barks
sharply and leaps at FRED to bite the seat of his pants)

FRED: Ow! (clutching himself he runs to HERBERT)Help!Help!

SAMMY: Careful, Wuffles.

HERBERT: Go on, you're not afraid of dogs, are you?

FRED: Yes.

HERBERT: (contemptuously) Huh! (moves to WUFFLES)

(WUFFLES jumps towards HERBERT snarling)

HERBERT: (running behind FRED) So am I.

SUSAN: I think Wuffles wants us to go home.

WUFFLES: (nodding sharply) Wuff.

SAMMY: Coming, Wuffles.

(They move L, WUFFLES retreating backwards, keeping an eye on
ROBBERS)
Sorry we can't come to tea today. Perhaps your mum will ask us again.
Bye-bye.

SUSAN: Bye-bye.

ROBBERS: (giving a nervous little wave, keeping their eyes firmly
fixed on WUFFLES) Bye-bye.

(BABES exit L. As WUFFLES turns by exit to follow them -)

HERBERT: (making long nose, quietly) Yah!

(WUFFLES turns and barks sharply. ROBBERS clutch each other.
WUFFLES stalks off L. contemptuously and they release each other)

HERBERT: Well, that didn't do us much good, did it?

FRED: It certainly didn't do me any good. Being bit like that
has set my nerves all a jangle.
(BARON pokes his head on R.)

BARON: Hist!

(FRED jumps)

HERBERT: What?

(BARON comes onstage)

Oh, I thought that was me over there for a moment. You mustn't say "hist" like that, Baron. You'll get us mixed up.

BARON: Haven't you done it yet?

HERBERT: No.

BARON: Well, I wish you'd hurry up. I need their lolly.

FRED: (producing a lollipop) You can have a suck of mine, if you like.

BARON: Thank you. (starts to lick it, then stops, annoyed with himself) I'm talking about money. Now look, I'll show you how to get into the house and you can do the job tonight.

HERBERT: Tonight? Oh, I don't think we can manage that.

FRED: No, there's all that homework teacher set us.

HERBERT: Besides it looks as if it might come on to rain later and you wouldn't like us to get the Babes wet, would you?

BARON: I don't care how wet they get. The dirty deed must be done tonight. (moves L.)

ROBBERS: (going with him) Oh, all right.

FRED: But don't blame us if they catch their deaths just before we murder 'em.

(They exit L. Enter ROBIN and MARION R.)

MARION: I don't think you'd better come any further, Robin. I'm afraid the Baron doesn't like you. But thank you for seeing me home.

ROBIN: Thank you for letting me. I'm sorry you have to go so soon.

MARION: Well, the Babes will be waiting for me. They like me to tell them a story before they go to bed.

(Enter BABES L.)

SUSAN: Are you coming, Marion?

SAMMY: Oh, hullo, who's this?

MARION: Robin H - I mean, the new blacksmith.

BABES: How do you do, Mr. Robin?

SAMMY: I think I'll be a blacksmith when I grow up.

SUSAN: You can't, that's what I'm going to be. Polly's promised to teach me.

SAMMY: All right then, I'll be - er - I know, I'll be a knight, then you can make me my armour, Susie. Do you make much armour, Mr. Robin? I expect you know lots of knights.

ROBIN: Well, I know a story about a couple of them.

BABES: Oh, tell us, please.

ROBIN: All right.

(BABES and MARION sit in a group L. Close traverse tabs during number and fly out cloth)

MUSIC 28. "JOUST A MOMENT"

(If feasible a guitar accompaniment is very suitable for this number)

ROBIN: I'll tell you a tale of the days of old,
When men were men and knights were bold.

"Ho, bring me my spear", cried Sir Eggwhite the
                                 Whisk,
"And polish my mail, and above-all be brisk;
Pour into my visor yon stuff in yon jug,
For I go to joust with Thir Thickneck the Thug".

BABES: More, more, tell us more;
This is the story we've been waiting for.

ROBIN: He drank sev'ral gallons of ale at a draught,
His steed went bow-legged in front, knock-kneed aft.
His squire quickly button'd him up with a spanner
And he went to the fray in a twice-nightly manner.

BABES: More, more, tell us more;
This is the story we've been waiting for.

ROBIN: Thir Thickneck led off with a mace to the jaw.
Sir Eggwhite replied with the cleaver -

MARION: Square Four!

ROBIN: The next bit of fight is not clearly defin'd
For Thir Thickneck went on but his horse stay'd
                             behind.

But nothing could stop bold Sir Eggwhite's advance;
He went at Thir Thickneck full tilt with his lance -
He's out for the kill! But the Thug saw him come
And dealt him a thundering thwack on the tum!

Sir Eggwhite the Whisk sail'd clean out of his
                             armour.
He landed in Kent, and was found by a farmer -

MARION: That was lucky, 'cos nothing else rhymes!

ROBIN: Thir Thickneck has triumph'd! And hear the crowd
                             cheer!

BABES: 'Ooray!

ROBIN: The moral is simple -

BABES & MARION: We've got it -

ALL: BEWARE OF TINN'D BEER!

<u>BLACKOUT</u>

Scene Five. THE NURSERY

(Fullset. Flats or cloth along front of rostrum to give nursery backing. Nursery wing with practical door L, nursery wing with practical door R, light switch on downstage side of door. Double bed L.C, towel on foot of bed. Single bed R.C. towel on foot of bed; nightgown, bedsocks and mobcap on top end. Table between beds with very large castor oil bottle, vast spoon and a bag of sweets on it. Waterproof cloth downstage of beds in C. Chair D.L. with socks on it. One sock has very large hole and darning wool and needle in it. Stage darkened to begin.

(EFFECT 6. THUNDER. LIGHTNING FLASHES. MUSIC 29. A candle appears round R.door followed by HERBERT's head)

HERBERT: Hist!

(FRED's head appears above his)

FRED: Hist, hist!

(In saying it he blows candle out. They come onstage. They are now in their Robbers' costumes again)

HERBERT: Now look what you've done, putting those extra hists in. My hist was quite enough.

FRED: Sorry.

HERBERT: Where are the matches?

FRED: (taking out box) Here they are. (strikes one, it doesn't light, strikes another failure) I think they've got damp with all this rain. (strikes a third, it lights) Ah, this is a good one. I'll save this. (blows it out and puts it in box)

HERBERT: Give 'em to me!

(He takes box, FRED leans on D.S. side of door as he lights candle. LIGHTS UP TO FULL)

Hm, very strong candle this.

FRED: Yes, and the funny thing is it happened just as I pushed down this little thing by the door here.

HERBERT: Well, no wonder, that's the light switch, you fool. (blows out candle)

(EFFECT 7. THUNDER. LIGHTNING FLASHES)

FRED: I wish this storm would give over. It's bad for my nerves, you know.

HERBERT: Never mind your nerves. What about our clothes? Sopping. As the Babes aren't here yet let's find a fire or something to dry 'em off. (moves to L.door and peers through it) All right, nobody around, come on.

(They exit L.)

MUDDLES: (off R) Right, left a little, more left, right.

NURSE: (staggering in backwards R with a large tin bath) Right?

MUDDLES: (off R) No, <u>left.</u>

NURSE: Well, make up your mind.

MUDDLES: (off R) All right, left. Now then, to you from me.

(NURSE falls backwards onto single bed holding bath. MUDDLES enters, dusting his hands and stands beside her)

There, we're through.

NURSE: (rising) Yes. (takes on seeing him beside her) Here, you're supposed to be holding the other end.

MUDDLES: Well, I said to you from me.

NURSE: Yes, but I didn't think you meant quite as much to me.

(She moves round to front of beds knocking MUDDLES down with bath, and places it on waterproof sheet)

There we are.

(They take two bars of soap, two scrubbing brushes, two mops and a wash board from bath)

MUDDLES: I thought you were going to bath the Babes, not scrub the floor.

NURSE: Oh, I always wash them really thoroughly.

(BABES enter R in their pyjamas, SAMMY with a candlestick)

Ah, we're just getting your bath ready, dears.

BABES: Oh dear.

NURSE: Now, now, no nonsense. Run and brush your teeth while Muddles and I fetch the water.

(She and MUDDLES exit R)

SUSAN: Oh, it is mean of Nurse to make us have a bath.

SAMMY: I tell you what, let's hide under the bed.

SUSAN: Oh, yes!

(SAMMY puts candlestick on table and they run and hide under double bed. HERBERT pokes his head round L. door)

HERBERT: Hist!

FRED: (poking head round and speaking into HERBERT's ear)
Hist!

HERBERT: (wiggling finger in ear) Desist! Come on, there's still nobody here.

(They enter, now in shirts, pants and socks only)

HERBERT: Bit of luck finding that airing cupboard.

NURSE: (off R) Come on, Muddles!

HERBERT:	Somebody coming! Hide!
FRED:	(dithering round in a circle) Where?
HERBERT:	(panicking around) Er - er - (sees bath) In here! Quick!
FRED:	Why? I'm not dirty.
HERBERT:	Get in!

(They get into bath crouching down. NURSE and MUDDLES enter R carrying two buckets of water each, which they take to bath)

MUDDLES: Where are the Babes?

NURSE: Still brushing their teeth, I suppose. Pour the water in.

(Each pours a bucket into the bath. ROBBERS sit up with a startled yelp, as NURSE and MUDDLES turn away to pick up their other buckets)

And the next lot.

(They pour the buckets in without seeing ROBBERS until they have finished)

MUDDLES: Well I never, they were here all the time.

NURSE: Fancy! Let's wash 'em then. Faces first.

(They pick up mops, dip them into bath and push them into ROBBERS' faces and waggle them round. NURSE works on HERBERT and MUDDLES on FRED)

Now their ears.

(They do their ears with the mop handles, using them like billiard cues)

And now a good scrubbing all over.

(They pick up scrubbing brushes and turn away to soap them. As they turn back ROBBERS rise)

ROBBERS: No!

NURSE & MUDDLES: (pushing them down again with a hand each on top of their heads) Yes!

(They scrub their hands, their arms, their chests and then yank up a leg each)

MUDDLES: They haven't taken off their socks.

NURSE: We'll have to wash their socks as well then.

(They scrub the soles of their feet and ROBBERS giggle hysterically)

MUDDLES: (holding up wash board) What's this for?

NURSE: Their backs, of course.

(She puts it between ROBBERS, who are back to back. Grasping them by the hair they pull them up and down on the board. During this the BABES come out from under the bed and move down one to beside NURSE and one to beside MUDDLES)

All over. Now wasn't that lovely?

(ROBBERS nod weakly)

NURSE: We'll dry them now, Muddles.

(BABES get towels off beds)

MUDDLES: Where are the towels?

(BABES hand them towels)

NURSE &
MUDDLES: Thank you.

(They take on the BABES and double-take on ROBBERS)

HERBERT: Vamoose!

(ROBBERS leap out of bath, scissor-crossing each other, HERBERT to R., FRED to L. BABES sit on ends of beds. NURSE moves R., MUDDLES L. They bump into each other, disengage and turn to chase ROBBERS. FRED and HERBERT circle upstage, scissor-cross again U.C. and NURSE and MUDDLES following them crash into each other U.C. and fall as HERBERT dashes out of L. door and FRED out of R. door)

NURSE: I wonder who they were?

FRED: (dashing back from R. to L.) Sorry, wrong way.

(NURSE and MUDDLES look after him in astonishment, then rise. During ensuing scene MUDDLES puts buckets, etc., in the bath and pushes it off R., then moves beside double bed)

NURSE: Anyway, I can't very well bath you now, dears, the water's all dirty.

BABES: Oh dear, what a pity. (they laugh and get into double bed)

NURSE: Yes, I thought you'd think that. But don't be too quick getting into bed. You haven't had your castor oil yet.

BABES: Oh, no, Nurse.

NURSE: Oh, yes, Babes.

(She picks up bottle and spoon. BABES look at them in distaste)

Who's going to be first?

(BABES exchange a look and dive under bedclothes pulling them over their heads)

Oh, they are naughty, Muddles. Fish 'em out again.

MUDDLES: (trying to pull clothes back) Come on, Babes, nice medicine. Lovely castor oil. Um - scrumptious, come on.

(There is a good deal of flailing about on the bed and eventually he manages to pull the clothes back and expose their feet. Their grinning faces come out of bottom end)

MUDDLES: I say, they have changed.

NURSE: They must be down this end.

(BABES immediately pull clothes over their faces as NURSE and MUDDLES move to pull back clothes at bottom end and BABES retreat up bed)

NURSE: After 'em!

(NURSE and MUDDLES go under clothes head first at bottom end and work their way up bed. BABES get out at top end. NURSE and MUDDLES come out at top, sit up, look round and see each other with a start of surprise. BABES have crept down to hide at foot of bed and now bob up)

BABES: Boo!

(NURSE and MUDDLES leap forward on bed. BABES dodge aside L.& R. so that they land on floor at foot of bed. BABES get into bed and look very innocent. NURSE and MUDDLES, a little dazed, turn and see them. BABES laugh)

NURSE: Oh, you are little tykes.

(She and MUDDLES rise)

Now, no more skylarking. You must have your castor oil. (pours a spoonful out) And I tell you what, I'll give you a sweetie afterwards.

BABES: Um, two sweeties.

NURSE: (firmly) One sweetie. It doesn't taste all that bad. Does it, Muddles?

MUDDLES: Oh, no.

BABES: Well, you have some then.

MUDDLES: Ye - eh?

NURSE: That's a very good idea. Muddles will show you how to take it.

(His mouth is agape and NURSE pours the spoonful into it. He gulps and remains deadpan)

You see. Muddles didn't mind it.

(MUDDLES pulls a ghastly face and with his tongue hanging out and coughing and spluttering, rushes off L.)

Silly boy, he didn't wait for his sweetie. Now it's your turn.

SAMMY: All right. I'll go first. (holds his nose)

NURSE: Good boy.

(She gives him a spoonful and his face wrinkles up in disgust)

And there's a sweetie. (pops a sweet into his mouth and pour out another spoonful) Now Susie.

(SUSAN holds her nose and reacts like SAMMY to her spoonful)

And there's a sweetie for you. (pops sweet into SUSAN's mouth and pours another spoonful) Now me. (holds her nose, swallows spoonful and splutters) Aah! What am I doing? Quick, where are the sweeties? (picks up bag and throws it away in disgust) There's none left!

(BABES laugh. She looks at them, then laughs too, their laughter building up)

NURSE: Fancy me taking it! And then - then there wasn't a
    sweetie!

(They whoop with delight, until NURSE suddenly stops, pulling a face)

It wasn't all that funny.

BABES: (stopping laughing) Oh, poor Nursie.

SAMMY: (offering it to her from his mouth) I've got a bit of mine
    left if you like.

NURSE: (eyeing it askance) Thank you, dear, but I won't rob you.
    (pushing his hand to his mouth) Pop it back. Now lie down so's I can
    tuck you up nice and comfy.

BABES: But we don't feel tired.

NURSE: I know, dears, but I do, so lie down.

    (They do)

    That's it. (she tucks them up on each side and kisses them, finishing
    on L. of bed) Nighty-night, darlings.

BABES: Nighty-night, Nurse.

NURSE: Sleep tight.

    (They grunt. She looks at them fondly and sighs)

    Now where's me darning? (sits on chair) Ouch! (pulls it from under
    herself) I've found it. What's the matter with this sock. (puts hand
    into it and her fist comes through large hole in heel) Oh dear. Sammy's
    that hard on his clothes, you know.

BABES: Nurse.

NURSE: Yes, dears?

BABES: (bobbing up) We still don't feel tired.

NURSE: Oh dear, oh dear, what am I to do with you?

SUSAN: Tell us a story.

NURSE: All right. Once upon a time there was a Prince and a
    Princess who'd never met each other and they never did so they lived
    happily ever after, now go to sleep.

SUSAN: Oh no, Nursie, tell us a proper story.

NURSE: Very well, then. But only if you'll promise to lie down
    and go to sleep.

BABES: All right, Nursie. (they lie down)

NURSE: That's good little children. What shall I tell you a story
    about?

SAMMY: About you.

SUSAN: Yes, when you were little.

NURSE: Oh, that's a <u>very</u> long time ago. I'm not sure I can remember all that far back. Still, I'll try. Are you lying comfortably?

BABES: Yes.

NURSE: Then I'll begin. (she darns quietly during number)

   MUSIC 30. "MANY YEARS AGO"

(Words and music by John Crocker, arr., Eric Gilder)

NURSE: When I was a little girl, many years ago,
I liv'd in a little house, so tiny and so low,
  With six brothers and six sisters,
  Why, we'd hardly room to grow,
But wé were oh! so happy there those many years
             ago.

When I was a little girl, many years ago,
My hair was so very straight, with ne'er a wave to
            show.
  I tried crimping, I tried curlers,
  But it still resembl'd tow -
And really it's no better since those many years ago.

When I was a little girl, many years ago,
My boy friend said, "Marry me, come to the church
            let's go"
  But we didn't, 'cos we wouldn't,
  We were only nine or so -
And no one's made the offer since those many years
            ago.

When I was a little girl, many years ago,
I liv'd in a little house, so tiny and so low,
  With six brothers and six sisters,
  Why, we'd hardly room to grow,
But we were oh! so happy there -
Oh, so very happy there -
How I wish that I was there - those many years ago.

Ah, they're asleep. Pleasant dreams, my loves. (sighs) They're very sweet, aren't they? Course, they're a bit naughty at times, I grant you, but - well, I like children to be naughty. I mean, it's natural, isn't it? (yawns and crosses to single bed) I shan't be sorry to get into me own bed either. (pulls back covers then removes her top clothes and releases her corset with a deep sigh of satisfaction) Oh, the relief! (scratches her tummy) Ah, lovely, lovely. I've been wanting to do this all day. (puts on nightgown, mob-cap and bedsocks) Now, me favourite moment. (puts her hands together in front of herself as if about to dive)

(WUFFLES trots in R. and rubs himself against her leg. NURSE puts hand down to scratch her leg, then prepares to dive again. WUFFLES rubs against her leg once more and she looks down)

NURSE: Wuffles, what are you doing in here?

(WUFFLES jumps onto foot of bed)

NURSE: No, no, Wuffles, you know that's not allowed. You've got your lovely kennel outside, haven't you?

(WUFFLES nods)

Well, you run and get into it.

(WUFFLES shakes head and snuggles down on foot of bed)

Now, now, come along. Out you go.

(WUFFLES slinks off bed, goes to door, turns and looks pleadingly at her)

Good dog, into your kennel.

(WUFFLES departs rather sorrowfully)

NURSE: He's a lovely dog, but I have to be firm with him, you know.

(again prepares to dive) Now then.

(EFFECT 8. CLATTERINGS AND BANGINGS OFF R.)

Oh, whatever is all that noise?

(Enter WUFFLES R.pushing a kennel before him. It has his name over opening)

Wuffles, you naughty boy. Take that out immediately. Go on.

(WUFFLES pulls a hot water bottle out of kennel)

Oh. Oh, that is nice of you, Wuffles.

(WUFFLES puts bottle in her bed)

Thank you, Wuffles. All right, you can stay.

(WUFFLES gives joyful bark and leaps into bed)

Oi, not in there, though. Out.

(She pushes him out and he jumps in again)

I said out.

(WUFFLES indicates that there is plenty of room for two)

NURSE: (shrugs) Oh, all right, we'll share it. (gets in on R side) Night-night, Wuffles.

(WUFFLES grunts. Slight pause. WUFFLES turns over and pushes her out)

Mind out! (goes round to other side of bed and squeezes into small space left to her)

(WUFFLES turns over and pushes her out that side)

(sighs) I don't know why I bother really. This happens every night, you know.

(She rises and picks up candlestick from table, crosses and works switch at R. door. LIGHTS DOWN TO HALF. She gets into kennel hind foremost)

NURSE: Ooh, what's this? (brings out a small lampost) Eh? Oh, yes. (puts it under WUFFLES' bed) Night-night.

(She blows out candle. LIGHTS DOWN TO QUARTER. She settles down with head resting on her arm. Pause. We hear little sighs from BABES, doggy whimpering from WUFFLES, then full blown snores from NURSE, all of which subside. MUSIC 31. HERBERT's head appears L)

HERBERT: Hist! (speaking back to FRED) All quiet, come on. We'll nab 'em now.

(They creep on)

You take that side and I'll take this.

(HERBERT moves to R of single bed and FRED to L)

Right, grab 'em!

(They grab and WUFFLES wakes up, barking furiously)

Quick, the other bed! (doubles round to L.side of double bed)

NURSE: Here, what's all the noise?)
BABES: What's the matter, Nurse?) (together)

(ROBBERS grab BABES and they scream)

NURSE: Where are the matches? What's going on?)
)
FRED: Ow! I've been kicked!   ) (together)
)
BABES: Help! Let go!   )

(ROBBERS struggle off with BABES L. WUFFLES is still barking)

NURSE: I've got you! It's no use struggling! Ow!

(She has managed to light two candles. LIGHTS UP TO HALF. She is holding them like a pair of pistols. WUFFLES has her seat firmly in his teeth)

NURSE: Let go!

(WUFFLES realises it is her and releases her)

(turning) Now, put your hands up or I'll set you on fire. Oh, Wuffles, it's you.

(She crosses and switches on lights. LIGHTS UP TO FULL)

What's the matter, did you have a bad dream? I hope you haven't woken the Babes. (looks at bed) The Babes! Where are they? They've gone!

(WUFFLES runs to and fro in a tizzy)

NURSE: (running first to R door then to L) Help! Help! The Babes! They've been stolen! Help! Help!

(MUDDLES dashes on L in nightshirt and nightcap. POLLY and MARION in nightdresses dash on R)

MUDDLES:	What's all the shouting about?)
POLLY:	Is there a fire or something?) (together)
MARION:	What's the matter, Nurse?)

NURSE: The Babes! They've disappeared!

MUDDLES:
POLLY &   Disappeared?!
MARION:

NURSE: Yes, stolen! Stolen! Oo-er! (faints into MUDDLES'
  arms)

MUDDLES: She's fainted! Wait a minute, I'll get you a pillow.
  (drops her and dashes to get pillow)

NURSE: Aah! (sits up)

MUDDLES: (returning with pillow) Here - (sees she is on floor)
  Oh.

NURSE: (bursting into tears) What are we going to do?

MUDDLES: Have a pillow.

NURSE: No thanks, I'm not hungry. Oh, what are we going to do?
  (bursts into further wails)

MARION &
POLLY: (comforting her) There, there.

  (Enter BARON R. in long dressing gown and nightcap R.)

BARON: Now then, what's all this hullabaloo? What, the Babes
  gone? Oh, no, no!

MUDDLES: How do you know they've gone? We haven't told you yet.

BARON: I read your thoughts. Anyway, they have gone, haven't
  they?

OTHERS: Yes.

BARON: (aside) At last, thank goodness. (to others) Oh, how
  terrible!

  (ROBIN dashes in R.)

ROBIN: Marion, are you all right?

BARON: What are you doing here, blacksmith? We don't want
  any horses shod.

ROBIN: I was passing and heard cries. I thought someone might
  be hurt.

MARION: Oh, Robin - the Babes have been stolen.

ROBIN: The Babes stolen? But by whom?

NURSE: I think it was two men, but I only heard their voices.

POLLY: Gypsies perhaps, there are some camped near here for
Nottingham Goose Fair tomorrow.

ROBIN: Whoever it was, I'll find them for you.

BARON: (contemptuously) You! What can you do by yourself?

(MUSIC 32. SCENE FINALE)

ROBIN: I have those who will aid me.
We'll start at the Fair tomorrow
And if we don't find them there
We'll search the length and breadth of England,
But find the Babes we will.

Where I shall lead many others will follow.
We will seek the children, break the chains
that bind them.
We'll search all England, the mountain-top and
hollow,
And we will never rest by day or night till we
find them!

BLACKOUT

Close traverse tabs.

(If resources are limited, it may be preferred to end the first part
here and cut scenes six and seven)

Scene Six. OUTSIDE STONEYBROKE HALL

(Tabs)

(BLUE FLASH L. BRING UP BLUE SPOT L. MUSIC 33. Enter
DEMON L)

DEMON:

    Aha, good friends, my schemes succeed,
    Toward their end the babes do speed;
    They'll search for them in vain, I trow,
    No mortal hand can save them now.

(MUSIC 34. BRING UP WHITE SPOT R. Enter FAIRY R)

FAIRY:

    Ye boast too soon of triumph's hour,
    Thou hast not yet usurp'd my power.
    The battle is but half begun.

DEMON:

    (aside) A plague upon this irksome one!
    (to her)
    What's this, good friend? I seek no strife,
    Ye know how blameless is my life.

FAIRY:

    I know thy life is foul with crime,
    Begone, thou hypocritic slime!
    Thy presence here doth taint the air.

DEMON:

    Thy hatred weighs me down with care,
    I'll go - and do what good I may.
    To help the Babes upon their way.

(He bows and exits L)

FAIRY:

    His good doth but betoken ill;
    E'en so, I shall defeat him still.
    'Tis only mortals can restore
    The Babes to those they love once more.
    But I can guard them safe from harm,
    So hence I'll Babes and Robbers charm
    And then with sleep bedew their eyes
    That here they'll stay till sun arise.

(MUSIC 35. FAIRY beckons to L with wand)

    Come - come, I say. I summon thee,
    I charge thee all, come here to me.

(Enter ROBBERS L, dragging unwilling BABES. FAIRY puts up her
wand and BABES will not be dragged any further)

    Stay there, sweet Babes, ye've earn'd your rest,
    Not one more step will ye be press'd.

(ROBBERS try pulling them with both hands, when this fails they try
cajolery, then another tug and then move behind BABES and try to
push them. FAIRY moves to BABES and touches each lightly with
wand. MUSIC TINGS on each touch)

    Now sleep thy senses will o'ertake.

(ROBBERS, puzzled what to do, stand scratching their heads. BABES
yawn hugely, stretch and go to sleep on each other's shoulders.
ROBBERS shake them. BABES indicate that they want to go to sleep.
ROBBERS shake their heads and point R. BABES shake their heads
and yawn again. FAIRY touches ROBBERS with wand. MUSIC TINGS
as she does so.

FAIRY   And thine.

(ROBBERS catch yawn from BABES, who again fall to sleep on each
other's shoulders. ROBBERS shake their heads trying to overcome
sleep)

                    Strive not to keep awake.

(ROBBERS yawn again and fall to sleep on BABES' shoulders.

          Now lie ye here.

(All lie down at L. side of stage)

                    And sleep ye well
          While I do cast another spell
          To stay awhile all evil schemes
          And fill thy thoughts with pleasant dreams.

(She waves wand. Traverse tabs open)

Scene Seven. THE LAND OF TOYS

(Fullset. (The precise setting and scope of the scene is left to the discretion of the producer to suit his own limitations and requirements)

(MUSIC 36. BALLET)

(A dream sequence in which FAIRY summons CHORUS who enter as various toys, dolls, etc. BABES get up and play with them in dance, and exit. ROBBERS join in a comic dance with some others of CHORUS and fall down again L, exhausted. DEMON enters with some naughty toys. They lie in wait for the BABES who re-enter with other toys. The DEMON and his followers try to make off with the BABES but are routed by the FAIRY leading the others. BABES lie down to sleep again beside ROBBERS)

CURTAIN

MUSIC 37. ENTR'ACTE.

PART TWO

Scene Eight. NOTTINGHAM GOOSE FAIR

(Fullset. Cut-out ground-row of fairground booths along back of rostrum. Steps down in C. Notices in C. of rostrum, "GRAND ARCHERY TOURNAMENT" pointing off L. "BOXING CHAMPIONSHIP" pointing off R. Fairground wing with sign "HAUNTED HOUSE" L. Fairground wing with sign "DANCING BEARS" R.)

(MARION and CHORUS discovered singing and dancing opening number)

MUSIC 38. "FUN OF THE FAIR"

MARION &
CHORUS:

Come and share the fun of the fair
    On Nottingham Goose Fair Day.
The stalls are shouting their merchandise,
With lots of bargains for greedy eyes,
    For more than you're able to pay.
Come and sample the festive air,
Take your turn at the side-shows there.
Come and stare at the things in the fair
    On Goose Fair Day.

(Enter ROBIN R)

MARION: Robin, any news of the Babes yet?

ROBIN: Not yet, I'm afraid. But I have my men all over the Fair. If they discover anything they'll report to me at once.

MARION: Well, I'm glad somebody's doing something. I can't get the Baron to do anything.

ROBIN: No, it's almost as if he doesn't want to find them. I wonder - No, never mind. I'm avoiding the Baron, anyway. He keeps pestering me to know when I'm going to "bring Robin Hood to him", and I don't want to arrest myself yet.

MUDDLES: (off R) Make way for the Sheriff!

ROBIN: Here he comes now. Let's slip away.

(They exit L. Enter MUDDLES R with long staff)

MUDDLES: Make way for the Sheriff, make way - (trips over staff)

(CHORUS laugh)

That's the third time I've done that. I must get the hang of this thing. (marching round stage placing staff down with every third step, e.g., left, right, left, right, left, right, etc.) One, two, three. One, two three. Got it. One, two, three.

CHORUS: (joining in behind him) One, two, three.

(The counting, led by MUDDLES, becomes quicker, so that he breaks into a quick waltz time and starts to dance, using the staff as his partner. CHORUS, laughing, also start dancing)

MUDDLES: One, two, three. One, two, three, de diddle de dum, de dum, de dum, etc.

(Enter BARON R.)

BARON: What the - ?

(Two of CHORUS cannon into him and knock him over)

You clumsy oafs!

(CHORUS stop dancing hurriedly and sheepishly. MUDDLES carries on
BARON rises and stands glowering at him, hands on hips, as MUDDLES
dances up to him not seeing him)

MUDDLES: De-dum, de-dum. (looks up to see who is blocking his
path and his voice trails away) De-dum - dum - dum - Hullo.

BARON: Do you come here often?   Anyway, where's my
announcement?

MUDDLES: Oh, that - yes. (takes up stance to L. of BARON and
bangs three times with staff) Pray silence for his self-importance,
the Sheriff of Nottingham. (bangs three times again, third time on
BARON's foot)

(CHORUS laugh)

BARON: (holding foot in pain) Ow! Do be careful.

MUDDLES: Sorry.

BARON: (clears throat) Citizens of Nottingham, I am here -

MUDDLES: (crossing legs and leaning on staff) They can see that.

BARON: I know they can.

MUDDLES: Then why tell 'em?

BARON: I wasn't telling 'em that I was here. I was -

MUDDLES: Ooh, you fibber, you were.

BARON: No, I wasn't.

MUDDLES: Yes, you were.

BARON: I wasn't.

MUDDLES: You were.

BARON: Shut up!

(He kicks foot of staff. MUDDLES falls down)

MUDDLES: (rising) There's no need to get rough. (crosses legs and
leans on staff again)

BARON: Well, don't interrupt then. (clears throat) Citizens of
Nottingham, I am here -

(He glares at MUDDLES, but MUDDLES is contemplating his finger-
nails)
today -

MUDDLES: Well, we didn't think you were here tomorrow.

BARON: Look, who's making this speech?

MUDDLES: You are.

BARON: Very well then, let me get on with it.

MUDDLES: I'm not stopping you.

BARON: Yes, you are.

MUDDLES: No, I'm not.

BARON: You are.

MUDDLES: I'm not.

BARON: Shut up!

(He kicks foot of staff and MUDDLES falls again)

MUDDLES: (rising) That's the second time you've done that. (crosses feet and leans on staff)

BARON: Be quiet! (clears throat) Citizens of Nottingham, I am here, today -

(Glares at MUDDLES, but MUDDLES is busy brushing specks of dust from the front of his jacket)

in order to open the Fair.

MUDDLES: But it's already been open for hours.

BARON: Of course it has, but I'm opening it officially.

MUDDLES: That's silly.

BARON: No, it isn't.

MUDDLES: Yes, it is.

BARON: It isn't.

MUDDLES: It is.

BARON: Shut up!

(As he kicks at foot of staff MUDDLES moves it over to other side so BARON falls by his own momentum. CHORUS laugh. BARON pulls his hand down his face in suppressed rage and frustration)

And you're the man who's supposed to be helping me. (rises) One more peep out of you and I'll - I'll -

MUDDLES: But I -

BARON: (clamping hand over MUDDLES' mouth) Shut up! (very fast) Citizens of Nottingham, I am here today in order to open the Fair. Don't miss the Boxing Contest, the Grand Archery Tournament or the many other exciting attractions because I get a rake-off on all of 'em. And so, without further ado, I now declare Nottingham Goose Fair open. Whew! Well, what about a few cheers then? Muddles, you lead them.

MUDDLES: I can't with your hand over me mouth.

BARON: Oh. (jerks hand away) Right, carry on.

(The following very flat and quick:-)

MUDDLES:	Hip-hip -
CHORUS:	Hurray.
MUDDLES:	Hip-hip -
CHORUS:	Hurray.
MUDDLES:	Hip-hip -
CHORUS:	Hurray. Can we go and enjoy ourselves now?
BARON:	Sometimes I feel I'm not appreciated. All right, buzz off.

(CHORUS exit L. & R)

MUDDLES: Well, that's that. (transfers staff back to R. hand and lands on BARON's toe)

BARON: Ow! (snatching staff) Give me that before you do any more damage with it. Now - (plonks it down on own foot) Ow! (throws it off) Where's Polly? She should be here by now. I've got a lot of money on her. I shall lose it if she doesn't get here in time.

MUDDLES: In time for what?

BARON: The boxing contest. I've entered her against the welter weight champion.

(HOUSE LIGHTS UP. Enter NURSE, WUFFLES and POLLY, carrying boxing gloves, at back of Auditorium. WUFFLES bounds ahead making friends with Audience, while the others make their way more slowly to the front)

NURSE: Here we are. I wonder which part of the Fair this is, Polly?

POLLY: I think it must be one of the sideshows.

NURSE: That's it, of course. These are the waxworks.

POLLY: Oh, yes. They're jolly good ones, aren't they? Quite lifelike.

NURSE: Yes, but you can see they're not really real. They've all got that glazed look in the eyes.

BARON: Oi! What are you doing down there?

NURSE: Ah, there you are. We're having a look at the waxworks.

MUDDLES: But those aren't waxworks down there.

NURSE: Are you sure? (peering over into orchestra pit) This looks very like the Chamber of Horrors.

POLLY: Ooh, maybe they're right, Nursie. Some of these waxworks can move.

NURSE: Dear me, how odd. (to one of Audience) Excuse me, madam, but you are a dummy, aren't you? No. Oh, I do beg your pardon.

BARON: You're the dummies. Come up here.

NURSE: Yes, I think we'd better.

(They move to catwalk. WUFFLES and POLLY cross onto stage)

I'll cover the rear. Ta-ta, so nice to see you. Sorry about our little mistake. Quite a natural one, of course - I mean - oh dear, that was an unfortunate slip. (trips and falls onto stage at end of catwalk)

(HOUSELIGHTS OUT)

Oops! so was that. (crawls on knees to others) Never mind, I made it. (looks up at POLLY) Have you grown suddenly or am I standing in a hole? (lifts skirts slightly to look) Aah! Me legs! Where are me legs?

MUDDLES: You're kneeling on 'em.

(WUFFLES points to them)

NURSE: Eh? Oh, so I am. (rises) Silly me. I knew I started out with them.

POLLY: Any news of the Babes yet, Muddles?

(WUFFLES starts looking round and wanders off L)

MUDDLES: No, nobody I've asked has seen any sign of them.

NURSE: Of course, you know where we ought to ask. In the pubs.

MUDDLES: But the Babes are too young to drink.

NURSE: Silly, I mean somebody may have heard something there. You know what places for gossip pubs are.

BARON: Hm, I wouldn't mind doing a bit of that kind of looking myself. Are they open?

NURSE: (smacking lips) Well, they feel as if they are. (looking for it) Where's me little watch?

WUFFLES: (off L) Wuff-wuff! (enters L carrying a very large watch in his mouth)

NURSE: Ah, thank you, Wuffles. Now let's see. (displays watch-face, which has "THEY'RE OPEN" where 12 would be and "THEY'RE SHUT" where 6 would be, and a single hand now pointing to "THEY'RE OPEN") Yes! Where's the nearest one, Wuffles?

(WUFFLES sniffs and turns head to R)

NURSE: Lead on!

(WUFFLES runs off R, with NURSE and BARON close behind. POLLY puts on boxing gloves)

MUDDLES: Don't you want a drink, Polly?

POLLY: Oh, no, Muddles. I'm in training. Got to keep fit for the fight, you know. (executes some boxing passes)

MUDDLES: (moving head L to avoid blow) Yes. (moving it R) All right. (ducks) Careful!

(As he comes up again she hits him and knocks him over)

MUDDLES: Ow!

POLLY: Oh, Muddles, I'm so sorry. I got carried away.

MUDDLES: (rising) If you go on like that I shall be too. (waggles his jaw, it sticks on one side) Oh, dear, I think you've broken it. I can't get it back.

POLLY: Here, let me try. (pushes at it)

MUDDLES: Ooh - ah - OOH!

POLLY: No good, I can't budge it. There's only one thing for it.

MUDDLES: What's that?

POLLY: This!

(She delivers a mighty blow to his jaw. He staggers back across stage and off L. **EFFECT 9. LOUD CRASH OFF L.** MUDDLES re-enters)

MUDDLES: I thought we were supposed to be friends. Why don't you take up something gentle like ... (whatever the latest dance craze is called) instead of boxing?

POLLY: Oh no, I couldn't. The Nott (or local reference) Glee Mad and Fo Soc would never forgive me.

MUDDLES: The Nott Glee Mad and Fo Soc?

POLLY: The Nottingham Glee, Madrigal and Folk Song Society. I'm their leading singer. It just so happens I have a selection from my repertoire with me. (takes out bundle of music) Which would you like to hear? (holds them out fanwise like a hand of cards)

MUDDLES: Er -

POLLY: This one. Right. (selects one and throws others off)

    <u>MUSIC 39.</u> "OLDE ENGLISHE DANCE(*)"

> A sweet pretty maid stood meek and shy,
> When a handsome youth came passing by.
> "He is strong and fair", quoth she;
> "I would that he would dance with me".
>
> And he said -

MUDDLES: Dance, dance, dance (*), sister!
Let's dance, dance, dance, Sister!
Let's dance, dance, the good old English dance, dance, dance!

(Enter CHORUS GIRLS and Female Principals as desired)

POLLY &
GIRLS: Hey nonny no, fa la la la la;
What strange music these words are!
Fa! La la, hey nonny no -
I think I'll up and have a go!

(Enter CHORUS BOYS and Male Principals as desired)

BOYS & MUDDLES:	Dance, dance, dance (*) etc.
GIRLS:	Hey nonny no, etc.,
BOYS:	Dance, dance, dance (*), etc.
ALL:	Dance, dance, dance (*) etc.

GIRLS and BOYS marked) (together)

(* Substitute the name of the latest dance craze for the word "dance" throughout)

(This production number can be built up as much as desired. At end of number all exit. <u>MUSIC 40.</u> BABES put their heads on L.)

BABES: Hist!

(They laugh and run onstage. They are still wearing their pyjamas. FRED hurries on after them)

FRED: No, no, no, I'm supposed to say that.

BABES: But we like saying it. (SAMMY on his R.and SUSAN on his L, into his face) Hisssssst!

FRED: (wiping his eyes) Look out! I got wet enough last night. Ooh, you're a proper handful you two. I don't think I can manage you by myself.

SUSAN: Where's Herbert gone to?

FRED: To buy you two some proper clothes. You're too conspic- uous like that.

SAMMY: Well, I hope he buys some food too, I'm jolly hungry.

SUSAN: So am I. Last night you said you were taking us on a picnic, but we still haven't had anything to eat.

FRED: Yes, I'm sorry about that, but we didn't expect to fall asleep. We thought we'd have done the - er - Here, I've got a bit of chocolate you can have. (produces it and gives it to them)

BABES: Ooh, thanks. (they break some off and eat it)

SAMMY: Don't you want a bit?

FRED: Well, I wouldn't mi - No, no, you have it.

SAMMY: All right, perhaps we'd better keep a bit for later, Susie.

FRED: Oh, you won't have a chance to eat it la - er - I mean - well, perhaps you're right.

SUSAN: I'll put it in here for safety. (puts chocolate in pocket of knickers)

SAMMY: Ooh, look! Dancing bears - let's go and see what they're like. (grabs FRED's arm and pulls him R.)

SUSAN: No, let's go into the Haunted House. (grabs FRED's other arm and pulls him L.)

FRED: Oi! Nark it! You'll split me in two! (they twirl him round and round)

FRED: Ooh! Stop! Me nerves are getting all twizzled up!

(They release him)

Anyway, we can't go into anything, I haven't any money.

SUSAN: It's not much fun coming to a fair and doing nothing.

SAMMY: I know, look, they're having a grand archery tournament. Well, we'll have a grand catapult tournament. (produces catapult and points off L.) You see that sign board down there? Whoever hits that is the winner.

SUSAN: What are we going to hit it with?

SAMMY: Er - (searches in pocket) This conker. You can have first go, Fred.

FRED: What, me? But these things are dangerous.

BABES: Oh, go on, Fred.

FRED: All right, but I don't like it. (averting his head fires conker off L.)

HERBERT: (off L.) OW! (enters holding nose with one hand and some clothes in the other) Who conked me on the conk with a conker? (sees catapult in FRED's hand and snatches it away) Really, Fred, you ought to know better, setting the children a bad example like that. (throws catapult D.L.) Now, here are some clothes for you. You put 'em on and let's get out of here.

WUFFLES: (off R.) Wuff-wuff.

SAMMY: That sounded like Wuffles.

SUSAN: (Looking off R.) It is Wuffles.

HERBERT: In that case, we'll get out of here immediately.

BABES: But we must wait for Wuffles.

ROBBERS: No, we mustn't. Come on!

(They hustle BABES off L. **MUSIC 41.** WUFFLES enters R.)

(WUFFLES trots to C., sits down, smacks his lips and wipes them in a satisfied way with paw, then sniffs, turns head to L. and sniffs again, rising. He nods, sniffs round in a circle, gives a triumphant bark and runs off L.

Sounds of cheering off R. MUDDLES, carrying stand with two bows and arrows, and BARON and MARION with POLLY wearing her boxing gloves between them enter R.)

BARON: (holding up POLLY's arm) Ladies and Gentlemen, the winner! Polly Flinders, the welter-weight wonder from ... (wherever is locally appropriate)

OTHERS: Bravo! Bravo!

(BARON moves away leaving POLLY's arm still up and MUDDLES moves into her side as two of CHORUS enter R. carrying a third on a stretcher, with boxing gloved hands dangling down on either side. They cross in front of group and exit L.)

POLLY: (peering down) Oh dear, I hope I didn't hit too hard. (lets hand drop onto MUDDLES' head)

MUDDLES: Ow! Yes, you did.

BARON: Well, you hit hard enough to win me a packet, anyway. Now, let's have the Grand Archery Tournament. (holding up a bag) There's ten golden crowns here and the first arrow in the gold wins the prize.

MUDDLES: (taking up bow and arrow and aiming it at bag) Oh, that's easy.

BARON: No, no, no, not this gold. The gold's what they call the centre of the target - down there. (points off L.)

MUDDLES: (peering off) Ooh, long way away, isn't it? Need a bow with telescopic sights for that. Still, here goes.

(He shoots arrow off L. Others look off L.)

Have I won?

MARION: I don't think so, Muddles. In fact, I can't see where it went at all.

MUDDLES: Ah well -
                    I shot an arrow in the air,
                    It came to earth I know not where.

NURSE: (entering L., indignantly) Well, I jolly well do. (turns to show arrow attached to her behind) Here!

MUDDLES: Oh dear, I suppose I get bottom marks for that. (pulls arrow off) Sorry, Nurse.

NURSE: Never mind, I'll have a go at this myself. (takes bow, fits arrow and points it at Audience) Where's the target? Out here?

OTHERS: No, no! It's there. (they point L.)

NURSE: Oh. (turns and aims off L.) Ah yes, should be able to reach that all right. (releases arrow so that it falls a few feet in front of her) Hm.

BARON: Disqualified. Next.

POLLY: My turn. (takes trick bow from stand, fits arrow, gives a tremendous pull and it breaks. Hinge on inside of bow, small flat cupboard bolt on outside, which POLLY pulls down) Oh dear.

BARON: Splendid. Nobody's the winner so I'll keep the prize.

ROBIN: (off R.) Stand back!

(All step upstage and look off R. EFFECT 10. "PING" OF BOW AND MUSIC WHIZZ. All heads turn sharply L.)

ALL: Hurray!

BARON: Confound it, somebody's won.

(Enter one of CHORUS, L., carrying a target with an arrow in the middle)

Slap bang in the middle. Who had the impudence to do that?

(Enter ROBIN R. with bow slung over his shoulder)

ROBIN: I did, Sheriff. May I have my prize?

BARON: That wretched blacksmith again, tcha! Take the money! (flings it at ROBIN) No! Give it back, I've forgotten to take out my commission.

ROBIN: (laughs and tucks bag in belt) Too late.

BARON: Curses! How dare you go around winning archery contests, anyway? You should be out hunting for Robin Hood. Today's your last chance to bring him to me, you know.

ROBIN: I have not failed you, Sheriff. Have you the hundred crowns reward ready?

BARON: (holding up a larger bag) Yes, but where is Robin Hood?

ROBIN: (bowing) Why, here, at your service, good Sheriff.

BARON: You!

ROBIN: None other. As you see I have kept my word, I have brought Robin Hood to you. Now you must keep yours! (sweeps bag of gold from BARON's hand)

BARON: You impostor! You thief! I'll have you hanged for this. Guards! Guards!

ROBIN: (blows horn) I shouldn't shout too hard, Master Sheriff, lest it cost you your life. Look.

(CHORUS as Merry Men enter L. with bows drawn and aimed at BARON)

BARON: (swallows) Guards, go away.

(WUFFLES runs on L. and tugs at NURSE's skirt, barking urgently)

NURSE: What's the matter, Wuffles?

(WUFFLES points L. and gives a series of barks as if speaking)

What? Oh yes, yes. Yes, yes. Yes. Ah!

MUDDLES: What's he say?

NURSE: I don't know.

(WUFFLES wags head frenziedly and scrathces head wondering what to do next. An idea strikes him. He points to himself then to his eyes, puts out a paw to indicate "one" and a second time to indicate "two", cradles his arms and ends by pointing dramatically off L.)

NURSE: I still don't know.

MARION: The Babes! That's what he means - he's seen the Babes.

BARON: (aside) Curses!

(WUFFLES nods vigorously and collapses L. in relief) } (together)

BARON: Ridiculous! I don't believe a wuff of it!

(WUFFLES notices catapult by his nose and jumps up barking and pointing at it)

NURSE: It's true! (picking it up) Look, here's Sammy's catapult.

ROBIN: (pointing L.) If they went that way they must be heading for Sherwood Forest. We'll scour every inch of it. Don't worry, Baron, we'll soon find the Babes now.

BARON: Oh - fudge and fiddlesticks!

ROBIN: Come men, off to the forest!

MUSIC 42. (Reprise 32)

Where I shall lead many others will follow.
We will seek the children, break the chains
that bind them.
We'll search all England, the mountain-top and
hollow,
And we will never rest by day or night till
we find them!

ALL: Hurray!

BLACKOUT

(Close traverse tabs, leaving NURSE and WUFFLES below them)

Scene Nine - NOWHERE IN PARTICULAR

(Tabs)

(LIGHTS UP AND NURSE AND WUFFLES are revealed)

NURSE:	Hurray! Hurray!	(together)
WUFFLES:	Wuff-wuff! Wuff-wuff!	

NURSE: (suddenly realising) Ooh, we've got left behind. Never mind, we'll catch up with them in a minute. I only hope we find the Babes, because I do miss 'em, you know.

(WUFFLES nods and points to himself)

NURSE: You too, eh, Wuffles? Tell you what then, I'll sing us a little song to cheer us up. Thank you, ... (Conductor's name) I think you'll like this, Wuffles.

MUSIC 43. "BOW-WOW!"

I've got a dog, he's a dear old chap,
When he was young he went YAP YAP YAP!
Then he went WUFF WUFF WUFF, and now -
Now he's a big dog - BOW-WOW!

That's a nice little song, isn't it?

(WUFFLES nods)

NURSE: I wonder if all these people would like to sing it, too? I say, would you like to sing?

(Audience reaction)

Well ...... (Conductor's name) said yes, but I didn't really hear anyone else, did you, Wuffles?

(WUFFLES shakes head)

I'll try again. Would you like to sing?

(She and WUFFLES encourage Audience to say "yes")

Ah, that's a bit better, but you can be a bit more definite about it than that. Would you like to sing?

(Audience reaction)

I think they would like to sing. I'm so glad because I spent a lot of time last night writing out the words. (turning upstage and calling up to Flies) Oi, Cyril (or whatever name is suitable) could I have the words, please?

(Song sheet comes down in front of NURSE and WUFFLES)

Blimey, the Audience has disappeared!

(She and WUFFLES peer round sides of song sheet)

Oh, there they are. Right, now altogether. One, two, three, four.

(She starts number then stops it)

NURSE: No, no, no, I said <u>all</u> together, like that last "yes" you did. Right - one, two, three, four. (leads them through song once) That was very nice, but I think they can do better than that, don't you, Wuffles?

(WUFFLES nods)

You can really let yourselves go on these. (points to words in capitals) We'll try them on their own. All ready for a good yap? Right - (leads them in saying "YAP YAP YAP") Not bad, try a bit harder though on the "wuffs". (leads them in saying "WUFF WUFF WUFF") That's more like it. Now bring the roof down with your "bow-wow". (leads them) Very good. Now let's do the whole thing as loud as that. One, two, three, four. (leads them through song again) Here, I've got an idea. As I haven't got my own Babes here to sing it with me, I wonder if some of you children would like to come up here and sing it? Wuffles, nip down and see if you can find a few.

(HOUSELIGHTS UP. WUFFLES goes over catwalk into Auditorium and helps up children. Ad lib with children until they have returned to their seats. HOUSELIGHTS OUT)

Right, now everybody again, last time so really belt it out. One, two, three, four -

(Fly song sheet as song is sung for last time. WUFFLES and NURSE wave as they exit)

BLACKOUT

(Open traverse tabs)

Scene Ten. THE DEPTHS OF SHERWOOD
FOREST

(Fullset. Cut-out ground-row of trees along back of rostrum. Cut-out of large forked tree in C.front of rostrum. Sloping ramp to stage in front of it. Tree wings L.& R. Leaves on either side of ramp)

(Enter ROBIN and CHORUS as Merry Men R)

MUSIC 44. REPRISE 16. "THE SPICE OF LIFE"

(ROBIN and CHORUS exit L. MUSIC 45. HERBERT's head comes round R.side of forked tree, FRED's comes round L.side)

ROBBERS: Hist! (they move to "Hist!" in C.of fork and bump heads) Ow! (they come from behind tree and down ramp onto stage)

HERBERT: Well, thank goodness they've gone. Now we can get on with the job.

(BABES' heads appear in C.of fork)

BABES: Can we come out too?

HERBERT: Yes, it's quite safe now, my little dears.

(BABES emerge, fully dressed again)

SUSAN: Are we going to have the picnic?

HERBERT: Well, - er - not exactly.

SAMMY: I know, let's play hide and seek. We'll hide and you seek.

(BABES run off above L.wing)

ROBBERS: (covering their eyes) Oh, yes!

HERBERT: (uncovering his eyes) No, no, no, what are we thinking of? We might lose you. (looks round) We have lost 'em! Quick, Fred, find 'em!

FRED: (looks blankly round) Where?

HERBERT: If I knew where we wouldn't have to find 'em, would we? Let's try over here.

(ROBBERS run to L.wing and start to go off above it and BABES start to come on below. ROBBERS move backwards onstage, BABES move backwards offstage. ROBBERS suddenly dash forward and off, BABES dash onstage and run off above R.wing. ROBBERS run on below L.wing and off above R.wing. FRED runs onstage below R.wing, stops, looks round and creeps back and off above wing. HERBERT pokes head round below wing, FRED above, they dive and grab each other, then realise they have only caught each other. BABES look on above L.wing smothering laughter)

Well, where are they then?

(BABES creep on to behind them, SAMMY behind HERBERT and SUSAN behind FRED)

HERBERT: (to Audience) Do you know where they are? What's that? Behind us? All right, we'll look behind us.

(ROBBERS turn inwards slowly until they are facing front again, BABES moving behind them)

ROBBERS: They're not behind us.

HERBERT: All right, we'll look again. We'll go the other way.

(ROBBERS turn outwards slowly and complete their circle, BABES again keeping behind them)

See, there's nobody there at all.

BABES: Boo!

FRED: Aah! (jumps into HERBERT's arms in fright) Oh, you shouldn't have done that. My nerves won't stand it. Look at me, I'm all of a tremble.

SUSAN: (running and hugging him) Oh, Fred, I do like you, you're such a baby.

FRED: Who me?

SUSAN: Yes, you sort of need looking after. I think I shall marry you when I grow up.

FRED: When you grow - Oh! (bursts into tears)

HERBERT: Fred, control yourself. How can we murder 'em with you blubbing like that?

BABES: Murder us?

HERBERT: Ooh, I'm sorry. I didn't mean to tell you like that, it just sort of slipped out. I was going to break it to you nicely.

SAMMY: You - you don't really mean it, do you?

SUSAN: Of course not. It's all a joke, isn't it, Fred?

(Slight pause, FRED shakes head glumly, HERBERT draws sword and sighs)

SAMMY: But why? Why should you murder us? We've never done you any harm.

HERBERT: It's not us that wants to murder you, sonny. We're doing it for your uncle.

BABES: Uncle?

SAMMY: Couldn't you just murder me and let Susan go?

HERBERT: I'm sorry, he was most particular it should be the two of you, otherwise he can't swipe your money. It won't take long and we'll be awfully gentle.

SAMMY: All right, then. We're not afraid to die, are we, Susie? (puts arm round her)

SUSAN: No. Well, only a little bit. Herbert?

HERBERT: Yes?

SUSAN: Will you let Fred murder me, please?

HERBERT: (huskily) Of course. (pats her head) Come, Fred.

FRED: (standing in front of BABES) No! I won't do it. I've grown too fond of 'em.

HERBERT: I've grown fond of 'em too, but business is business. And think, Fred, they're young, they'll get over it.

FRED: Yes, but I shan't, so I won't murder 'em.

HERBERT: Very well then, I'll do it by myself.

FRED: (drawing sword) No, you won't!

HERBERT: Fred, get out of my way!

FRED: Shan't! I'm a devil when I'm roused, and I'm roused now!

HERBERT: And so am I!

(He lunges at FRED with sword, FRED parries and retaliates and they start to fight in earnest)

SUSAN: Oh dear, I'm sure they'll hurt themselves in a minute.

SAMMY: (whispering) Never mind that, now's our chance, Susie - let's run for it!

SUSAN: Yes, but -

SAMMY: Come on, Susie!

(BABES run off L. MUSIC 46. Fight continues until they disarm each other simultaneously. They draw daggers and stalk each other and leap at one another, miss and fall on their faces losing daggers. HERBERT draws his pistol, FRED searches for his)

FRED: Where's me popgun? Lock the forest, I've lost me popgun.

HERBERT: Oh, sorry, I've got it. (gives it to FRED)

FRED·   Ta.

(HERBERT levels his pistol at FRED and pulls trigger, it clicks)

HERBERT: Blow, no bullet.

(FRED aims popgun at HERBERT and tries to fire it)

FRED: Dash, no cork.

(They turn them round to use as clubs, get together, grapple and HERBERT knocks FRED's popgun out of his hand and bonks him on head. FRED falls and HERBERT puts a foot on him, triumphantly. He holds the pose a moment, then looks down at FRED with misgiving)

HERBERT: Here, Fred, are you all right? (pause) Fred, are you all right, I say? (kneels beside him) Fred, speak to me. (raises FRED's head onto his knee) Speak to me, Fred!

FRED: I can't.

HERBERT: Why not?

FRED: I can't think of anything to say. (groans and sits up rubbing head)

HERBERT: Oh, Fred, I was afraid I'd done for you.

FRED: Here, where are the Babes?

HERBERT: Eh? (looks round) Ooh. They must have run off while we were fighting.

FRED: Oh dear, what are we going to tell the Baron?

HERBERT: Well, we'll just have to pretend we did it, otherwise we shan't get our money. We'll go back and report to him now.

(They start collecting up their scattered weapons)

FRED: But they're all out looking for us. How are we going to get into his house?

HERBERT: We'll disguise ourselves as workmen or something.

(Voices off R.)

FRED: Ssh! I thought I heard voices.

(More voices off R.)

HERBERT: You did, and what's more there's people talking. Quick, scarper!

(They run L.)

(stopping suddenly) Fred - I'm glad we didn't do it.

FRED: So am I.

(They run off L.)

NURSE: (off R.) Come on, Wuffles, you're supposed to be pulling me, not me you.

(Enter R., dressed as a policewoman dragging a rather tired WUFFLES on a leash. POLLY as a Brownie follows. WUFFLES flops down)

POLLY: Poor thing, I expect he's tired. Shall I carry him for a bit?

(WUFFLES thinks this is a good idea, nods vigorously and jumps up to be carried)

NURSE: No, no, no, we'll never train him to be a proper police dog if we mollycoddle him. Down, Wuffles.

(WUFFLES dejectedly gets down and goes to sleep)

Where's Muddles got to?

POLLY: He's still searching for footprints.

(Enter MUDDLES R, in Inverness cape and deer-stalker cap, with large curved pipe in his mouth, bending forward eagerly examining ground through a large magnifying glass)

MUDDLES: Yes, I'm on to something here - definitely human footprints. (focusing on NURSE's foot) Aha! what's this? A human foot! Does it fit the prints? (moves her foot to test it) It does! And this foot won't be lying around by itself, it'll be attached to somebody. (moving up NURSE with magnifying glass) Yes, I'm right. Ah, gravy for lunch. It must be one of the robbers, it must - (focuses onto NURSE's face) Oh.

NURSE: What do you think you're playing at?

MUDDLES: I'm following a trail. And I think I'm on their track all right - there are two sets of prints and they've got a dog with them.

POLLY: Oh, Muddles, those are our prints.

MUDDLES: Are they? I never thought of that.

NURSE: You leave the tracking to Wuffles. I'm teaching him to be a police dog.

MUDDLES: Is he any good?

NURSE: Marvellous, watch this. I'll show you how alert he is. He's ready to do anything at a whispered word of command. Watch. (whispering) Wuffles. Wuffles! Wuffles, wake up! WAKE UP!

(WUFFLES wakes with a start)

NURSE: That's better. We'll try scenting. Scent, Wuffles.

(WUFFLES looks puzzled)

Scent, boy, scent.

(WUFFLES thinks)

Oh, come on, Wuffles, you know what scent is.

(WUFFLES - an idea strikes him, he nods, then mimes holding a scent spray and using it behind his ears and under his arms)

NURSE: No, no, no, not that sort of scent.

POLLY: Like this, Wuffles. (gets on all fours and sniffs around)

(WUFFLES looks at her in amazement)

NURSE &
MUDDLES: Yes, like this.

(They get down like POLLY and all sniff moving L.)

WUFFLES: (follows them, even more astonished and taps head to AUDIENCE to indicate that they are mad. Suddenly smells something and sniffs the air) Wuff! (he runs ahead of them and onto catwalk, sniffing hard)

MUDDLES: He's found something!

POLLY: It must be the Babes!

NURSE:　　　　　After him, quick!

　　(WUFFLES moves over catwalk into Auditorium)

　　(HOUSELIGHTS UP. Others pause on catwalk)

NURSE:　　　　　Ooh, where's he going?

　　(WUFFLES moves to somebody who has chocolates and begs)

POLLY:　　　　　He's after their sweets!

NURSE:　　　　　Wuffles, you naughty dog, come back here!

　　(WUFFLES moves further into Auditorium)

　　(Others move into Auditorium)

　　Come here, Wuffles.

WUFFLES:　　　　Wuff! (runs out through a pass door)

NURSE:　　　　　Oh, I do hope you'll forgive him, trying to cadge sweets
　　like that. Of course, I'm rather partial to that kind meself.

MUDDLES:　　　　So am I.

POLLY:　　　　　And me.

NURSE:　　　　　But we wouldn't dream of trying to cadge, would we?

POLLY &
MUDDLES:　　　　Oh, no!

　　(All smack their lips rather pointedly)

NURSE:　　　　　What? Oh, how kind of you.

　　(WUFFLES runs onstage L)

WUFFLES:　　　　(shaking head reprovingly) Wuff-wuff!

ALL THREE:　　　Rumbled!

NURSE:　　　　　Quick, back again.

　　(They get back onstage. HOUSELIGHTS OUT)

　　That was very naughty of you, Wuffles, leading us astray like that. You
　　want to find the Babes again, don't you?

　　(WUFFLES nods)

　　Then you do some proper scenting.

　　(WUFFLES nods and puts nose down sniffing round in a little circle,
　　then stops. Sniffs hard and moves purposefully to L)

POLLY:　　　　　Is it the Babes, Wuffles?

　　(WUFFLES shakes head)

NURSE:　　　　　What is it then?

WUFFLES:　　　　(disdainfully indicates a cat washing himself) Meow.

ALL THREE:　　　Cats!

(WUFFLES nods)

BLUE FLASH L. BLUE SPOT UP L. <u>MUSIC 47.</u>

(DEMON leaps on L. hissing and adopting a menacing attitude. WUFFLES yelps and leaps into NURSE's arms. Others shriek. MUDDLES leaps into POLLY's arms. ALL run off R. DEMON laughs. START LIGHT FADE)

DEMON: Your pardon if I did affright,
                   My only purpose was their flight.
                   The Robbers bold their task did scorn
                   So I the Babes have hither drawn,
                   That I may this omission mend.
                   I'll bring the Babes to their fell end,
                   With bitter cold and biting frost.
                   See, they come - hungry, tired and lost.

(He backs off L. Enter BABES R)

SAMMY: Come on, Susie, I'm sure we'll find our way home soon.

SUSAN: Oh, Sammy, I'm so tired. Couldn't we rest a little?

SAMMY: All right, we'll stay here a bit.

(They sit on ramp)

I wish we had something to eat, though. I'm so hungry. (searches in pockets, brings out a conker) You can't eat conkers, can you? (brings out string) Or string. (brings out handkerchief) I wonder what handkerchiefs taste like.

SUSAN: Wait a minute, I've still got that bit of chocolate Fred gave us. (goes to pocket in her knickers) Oh dear, no good, it's all melted.

SAMMY: Well, I suppose it won't do us any harm to do without supper.

SUSAN: No, but I wish we hadn't had to do without breakfast, dinner and tea as well.

(SAMMY yawns)

Are you tired too, Sammy?

SAMMY: Me? Oh, no. But if you want to go to sleep for a bit, you carry on and I'll keep watch.

SUSAN: (shivers) Let's both go to sleep then we can huddle together to keep warm.

SAMMY: Well, perhaps I'll lie down, but I won't go to sleep. (yawns again)

(They lie down)

SUSAN: I wish Nurse was here to sing us to sleep.

SAMMY: (sitting up) I'll sing you to sleep, if you like. I only

SAMMY:	(continued) know one song, though.
SUSAN:	(drowsily) Sing it then.
SAMMY:	All right. (sings unaccompanied)

> Half a pound of tuppeny rice,
> Half a pound of treacle,
> That's the way the money goes -
>   Pop goes the weasel. (looks to see if she is

asleep)

> Half a pound of tuppeny rice,
> (his singing gets slower)
> Half a pound of treacle, (yawns)
> That's the way the money goes -
> (subsides to lying position)
> Pop - goes - the - um.

(END FADE. Slight pause. <u>MUSIC 48.</u> Enter DEMON L.)

DEMON: Now come ye icy blasts so cold -

<u>(EFFECT 11. WIND NOISE)</u>

> Let frost and snow their limbs enfold,
> Till they're past mortal hand to save
> And where they lie becomes their grave.

<u>(MUSIC 49.</u> Enter FAIRY R.)

FAIRY: Hold, evil one! Dost now deny
          That which is plain to ev'ry eye?

DEMON: Why, no, for now the prize is won,
          My day begins, thy day is done!

FAIRY: Thy lying words do seal thy fate,
          Now naught my anger shall abate.
          Villain henceforward from his hour
          I deem thee void of magic power!

(DEMON laughs. Music ting as she touches him with wand. His laughter breaks off)

DEMON: What's this? 'Tis true, my power goes,
          I feel it as away it flows.
          Curse thee, Fairy, curse thee, I say!
          Now all my hopes are gone astray,
          My cherish'd evil vanquish'd quite,
          Curse thee, thou sanctimonious sprite!

(He moves to strike her. She puts her wand up, he is powerless and slinks off L.)

FAIRY: And now the Babes must saved be.
          I with my birds from branch of tree,
          Will o'er these twain some leaves bestrew,
          That they may sleep the nightlong through,
          Warm and happy as Babes should sleep

FAIRY: (continued)
                    Till sunlight through the sky doth peep.

(MUSIC 50. BIRD BALLET. CHORUS as Birds enter L. and R. At end of ballet FADE LIGHTS UP FOR SUNRISE EFFECT. MUSIC 51)

                    Come now, thou valiant Robin Hood,
                    And end thy search within the wood.

(Enter ROBIN R.)

ROBIN: I'm sure I shall find them soon - something seems to draw me to this place. What's this? (moves to ramp and kneels) I have found them. And sleeping as softly as if they were in their own bed. Wake up, Babes, you're safe now.

(EFFECT 12. BIRD CALLS. MUSIC 52. "GREENSLEEVES". BABES yawn and stretch and rub their eyes as they sit up)

SAMMY: Where are we?

SUSAN: Oh, isn't it a lovely morning?

BOTH: Hullo, who are you?

ROBIN: I'm Robin Hood.

BOTH: Robin Hood!

SAMMY: Gosh! Please, can I be an outlaw?

ROBIN: (ruffling his hair and laughing) Maybe - someday. But now, you're going home.

SAMMY: Oh no, I'd much rather stay here with you, wouldn't you, Susie?

SUSAN: Well, there might be some breakfast at home.

SAMMY: That's true. Let's go home.

ROBIN: (taking them each by the hand) Come on then - home we go!

(Upsurge of music. Grouping of FAIRY and BIRDS as they move slowly off L. and traverse tabs close slowly. Fly in Scene Eleven frontcloth, if used)

Scene Eleven. STONEYBROKE HALL

(Frontcloth (Interior of Baronial Hall), or Tabs. If cloth is used, tabs to open as soon as convenient during scene)

MUSIC 53.

(Enter BARON L., staggering under the weight of a large black chest marked "SAMMY & SUSAN")

BARON: All their wealth in here and I daren't open it yet. Oh, the suspense is killing me - so's the weight. (lowers chest onto own foot) Ow! Surely those Robbers have done the job by now, or perhaps they've been caught and all is revealed. In that case I must fly with the money. (strains to lift chest) I must fly - uh ...I must - ah ... I must stay where I am. If only I knew whether the Babes were dead or not. I don't even know how much there is in here. Dare I take a peep? I dare. (tries to lift lid) Locked. Well, of all the distrustful little - perhaps I could prise it open. How lucky I always carry a hammer and chisel. (produces them) Now, gently. (bangs away with abandon at chest) Done it. Nobody would suspect it had been forced. Now, just one quick peep and shut again. (lifts lid, peeps inside and slams lid down, trapping head) Aah! That was too quick. Peep again. (lifts lid) Ah, lovely, lovely! All in jewels. But what sort of stones are these? (picking one up to examine it) They look just like ordinary pebbles to me. (finds paper in chest and reads it) "Dear Daddy's greatest treasure - his fossil collection". Curses! All this trouble for a few footling fossils. Fifty-five forbidden phrases! (slams down lid onto hand) Wow! (shakes hand and sucks thumb)

(Enter MARION and POLLY R.)

MARION: Hullo, Baron, what are you doing?

BARON: (hurriedly trying to hid box) Oh - er - er - nothing. (puts handkerchief on box)

MARION: Isn't that Susie and Sammy's?

BARON: This? (lifts handkerchief) Why, so it is. Well, I never. I wonder how that got here?

POLLY: I saw you struggling down from the attic with it just now, so I suppose you brought it.

BARON: Me? (aside) Curses, no privacy in this house. (to her) Oh, yes. So I did. I can't think why though.

POLLY: Neither can I. Everybody thinks they keep all their money in it, but they don't. That's in a small red box.

BARON: How very interesting. Excuse me, I must go and look for a small red box - I mean, some small red socks.

MARION: Aren't you going to take this back?

BARON: Well, I would, but I don't seem to be able to lift it.

POLLY: Oh, that's easy. (lifts it without effort) Catch! (throws it to him)

(BARON just manages to catch it, but the weight spins him round and spinning faster and faster he disappears off L. **EFFECT 13. GLASS CRASH OFF L.**)

POLLY: Why's he gone into the greenhouse with it?

MARION: Why did he want it at all? I don't think you should have told him about that red box, Polly. He'll turn the whole house upside down looking for it.

POLLY: That's all right. I bet he doesn't look in the one place it is.

MARION: Where's that?

POLLY: Underneath all those stones in the black box.

(They laugh)

MARION: Men are very simple really, aren't they?

POLLY: Well, they make a lot of fuss about everything, but they don't really do anything until we've sort of told them what to do.

MARION: And sort of made them think it was their own idea.

POLLY: In fact, I don't know why we bother with them.

MARION: Neither do I.

BOTH: Men!

MUSIC 54. "MEN!"

(Close traverse tabs slowly during number and fly out cloth)

BOTH: Men! We could strangle 'em, men make us
                                furious;
    Men are insensitive, rough and injurious.
        But when the lighting blows a fuse,
        We'd rather not do without men.

MARION: Girls decorate the place, girls are the pretty
                                ones;

POLLY: Men are all odds and ends, odd bobs and bitty
                                ones;

BOTH: But when the car's refus'd to start,
        We'd rather not do without men!

MARION: Men aver that they are intellectual!
    Quietly effectual,
        They say they are.

POLLY: Have you seen him in his early morning daze?
    Lord of all that he surveys?
        Ha! Ha! Ha!

BOTH: Men say such awful things, quite indefensible.
    Men we can do without, men are dispensable.

ot do without men!

BOTH: (continued)

But if you want to cuddle and kiss,
We'd rather not do without men!

(Dance)

We must protest at the way that they handle us.
Ideas that they suggest really are scandalous;
But if you want a family,
We'd rather not do without men!

BLACKOUT

(Open traverse tabs)

Scene Twelve. THE NURSERY

(Set as before but without previous furniture. Instead there is a long trestle table C, with rolls of wallpaper on it. Under table two mops, two buckets, some nails, two hammers and a toilet roll. Set of steps U.L. set of ropeless steps U.R.)

(MUDDLES is discovered behind table R, and NURSE L.)

NURSE: Now, we're all ready, but where are those two workmen I ordered to come and help us? We'll have to start without them.

MUDDLES: Are you sure it's worth redecorating the nursery for the Babes? I mean -

NURSE: Oh, yes, dear, I'm sure they'll be back. I feel it in my corset bones. Now, let's wash down the walls, dear. (picks up a mop and bucket)

MUDDLES: (picking up mop and bucket) But there isn't any water in these buckets.

NURSE: Well, we'll give 'em a dry clean then.

(They move up to back, elaborately dip mops in empty buckets, swirl them around and squeeze out imaginary surplus from them, then start vigorously mopping walls, working very quickly and singing as they do so. MUDDLES moves onto R, wing and NURSE onto L. MUSIC 55. The doors open and HERBERT's head appears R. and FRED's L.)

ROBBERS: Hist!

NURSE &
MUDDLES: (turning to each other) Beg pardon?

NURSE: Did you speak?

MUDDLES: No, did you?

NURSE: No.

BOTH: Oh.

(They return to their mopping and mop down ROBBERS without noticing them. ROBBERS sneeze and move out of sight)

(turning to each other) Bless you. Got a cold?

NURSE: No.

MUDDLES: Neither have I.

BOTH: Oh. (they move onto "fourth wall" and meet in C.)

MUDDLES: Very dirty bit here.

NURSE: No, no, no, that's the audience.

(They cross their mops on the imaginary wall so that they are mopping each other's faces)

BOTH: Look out! (they remove bits from their mouths)

NURSE: Well, that's that, anyway.

(They move up behind table and bend down to put away buckets and mops.
MUSIC 56. ROBBERS peer on again)

HERBERT: All clear yet?

FRED: All clear.

(They creep on to below C. of table. They are disguised as workmen in
overalls)

HERBERT: So far so good. Our disguise has worked. Now to find
the Baron and report to him.

NURSE &   (rising) Now, then -
MUDDLES:

(ROBBERS jump guiltily to L.)

Oh.

NURSE: You arrived very quietly. Anyway, where have you been?
You're late.

ROBBERS: Are we?

NURSE: Yes, you should have been here half an hour ago.

ROBBERS: Should we?

NURSE: Well, that's when you said you'd be here.

ROBBERS: Did we?

NURSE: Are we? should we? did we? What's the matter with you?

MUDDLES: I suppose they are the workmen we're expecting.

FRED: No.

HERBERT: Yes. (nudges FRED) What do you want us to do?

NURSE: We're just ready to start on the wallpapering.

FRED: Wallpapering? How do you do that?

HERBERT: Ssh! Leave it to us, madam, we're expert wallpaperers.

(NURSE and MUDDLES give to R. as ROBBERS move behind table)

Right, roll 'em out, Fred.

FRED: What - these bits of paper?

HERBERT: Yes, roll 'em out.

FRED: All right.

(He rolls the rolls still done up along table so that they fall off other end
where NURSE and MUDDLES catch them)

NURSE: What are you playing at?

HERBERT: I'm afraid my assistant's a bit new to the business.

FRED: So are you.

HERBERT: Ssh!

NURSE: (moving to C. of table) You should do it like this. You hold
one end then roll it out. (does so, so that it rolls back) Oh. Well, you
roll it out - (does so, and it comes back again) - like so and - oh. You
roll it out and quickly grab this end - (rolls it out, leaves go of R. end
and grabs L, so that R. end rolls up) - and then you can - oh! Well,
you put something to hold this end here - (puts a foot on L. end) - and
then you push this bit back here - (pushes it as far as she can till she is
spreadeagled along table) - and you're all ready to start pasting.
(rises, releasing both ends so that they roll together) Simple, see? Oh.
Here, you grab hold of this - (gives HERBERT the roll end of paper)
- and you grab hold of this. (gives FRED other end) Now pull it out.

(NURSE and MUDDLES move below table. HERBERT pulls to L. and
out of L. door, FRED to R. and out of R. door during following:-)

Now, Muddles, where's the brush and paste I asked you to get?

MUDDLES: (producing small pot of "Grip-Fix") Here's the paste.
And here's the brush inside it. (opens lid and brings out tiny brush)

NURSE: And how far round the room is that going to go?

MUDDLES: (looks round room then looks at little pot) Hm, I didn't
really think about that. It's very good paste, though.

NURSE: Ah well, we'll have to nail it up instead.

(They move up and walk through the paper stretched across the stage.
The broken ends move off-stage)

Ooh dear, now look what we've done. Stop 'em, quick.

(MUDDLES runs and puts his foot on R. piece and NURSE runs and puts
her foot on L. piece. Both pieces are pulled offstage which sweeps them
off their feet. They rise and run to doors)

BOTH: Oi! Come back!

NURSE: Oh, where have they got to?

(HERBERT appears moving backwards in R. side of Auditorium dragging
a long length of paper. HOUSELIGHTS UP)

HERBERT: Is this far enough?

NURSE: What are you doing down there?

HERBERT: Well, you said to pull it out.

NURSE: Come back here.

HERBERT: All right. (turns and makes his way backwards to catwalk dragging paper and onto stage)

(HOUSELIGHTS OUT when he is onstage)

NURSE: Now, Muddles, you can start nailing some paper up over there. (indicates R.wing and gives him nails and hammer) Now you want some paper. (picks up toilet roll) What's this doing in here? This is the one we're going to paper the bathroom with. (gives MUDDLES a small roll of wallpaper) Here you are, dear.

MUDDLES: But I can't reach up to the top.

NURSE: Well, use a pair of steps.

MUDDLES: Oh, yes.

NURSE: This man can help you and I'll use his bit of paper to start over here.

(She takes paper from HERBERT, moves steps by L. wing. HERBERT crosses and helps MUDDLES to open out the ropeless steps completely so that they are lying flat on the ground. MUDDLES walks along them to top step)

MUDDLES: I still can't reach.

NURSE: I'd no idea that pair were so low. Well, I'll let you have this pair in a minute.

(HERBERT and MUDDLES clear ropeless steps off. NURSE mounts her steps and lets paper roll down the wall)

Now then - oh, I've forgotten my hammer and nails. (lets paper drop, runs down steps, gets nails and a hammer and runs up steps) Silly me. Now I've forgotten the paper. (runs down, picks up paper and, holding it in front of her, mounts steps putting her feet through it at each step and only has a little torn off bit when she reaches the top) Hm, a trifle inadequate. Still, better than nothing. (holds it up to bang nail in and hits thumb) Ow! (comes down steps) Well, anyway that's one bit up. (takes the paper from steps and looks at it) This'll come in handy for going round light switches. (puts it under table)

(FRED appears in Circle or at back of Auditorium. HOUSELIGHTS UP as soon as he speaks)

FRED: How much further do you want me to pull this out?

NURSE: Blimey, I'd forgotten about him. It's all right, you can come back now.

(HOUSELIGHTS OUT. FRED leaves Auditorium)

We don't seem to be getting on very fast, do we? I'd like to get just one decent piece up.

MUDDLES: Wait till I get mine up then. (unrolls paper a little) No, that's the wrong way up. I want the other end. (unrolls it, dropping it over himself till he gets other end) Yes, this is the right way. Or is it? (drops the end he is holding and pulls the paper back a bit) Where's the first end?

HERBERT: Here it is. (picks it up and manages to coil it round MUDDLES)

MUDDLES: I've lost the other one again now.

NURSE: Well, it's here somewhere. (finds it) Here we are.
(manages to coil that round MUDDLES)

MUDDLES: But which is which?

NURSE: This was the first end.

HERBERT: No, this was.

NURSE: No, no, I remember because when he started this was here
and he threw it back here.

HERBERT: No, that was there and it was this he threw back here.

NURSE: Then this wasn't here, but there.

HERBERT: Or that was there and this was here.

(They have by this time thoroughly entwined MUDDLES so that he has
disappeared from sight)

MUDDLES: Oi! Help! Let me out, let me out! (battles his way out)

NURSE: Oh, Muddles, now you've ruined it.

MUDDLES: Well, I was suffocating.

NURSE: Now do let's get a bit of paper up.

(HERBERT clears the paper off. NURSE climbs steps. MUDDLES takes
a fresh piece of paper and hands it up to her. She unrolls it so that it
hangs down over L. door)

Right, I'll nail the top and you nail the bottom.

(She nails it to top of wing and MUDDLES to floor. NURSE comes down
steps)

There we are, and very nice too.

(As they stand admiring it FRED enters through L. doorway ripping the
paper)

FRED: Hullo.

HERBERT:
MUDDLES &   Oh, no!
NURSE:

NURSE: I give up.

MUDDLES: So do I.

HERBERT: So do I.

FRED: What are you giving up?

OTHERS: Work.

FRED: Oh, I gave that up years ago.

NURSE: You know, there's one thing you can be sure of - if you
want a good job done badly -

ALL: Do it yourself.

MUSIC 57. "DO IT YOURSELF"

ALL: If you want a good job done badly,
                            Do it yourself, say I.
                        Save up some dough and have a go,
                            And never say D.I.Y.

HERBERT: I once had a try at mending a lamp
                        And blew the main fuse in a blinding flash!
                        If you want a good job done badly -
                            Do it yourself!

NURSE, MUDDLES,   If you want a good job done badly, etc.
& FRED:

NURSE: I rewasher'd a tap and made a slip
                        And the water flow'd in with a splish, splosh,
                                                        splash!

HERBERT: And blew the main fuse in a blinding flash!

NURSE &   If you want a good job done badly -
HERBERT: Do it yourself!

MUDDLES &   If you want a good job done badly, etc.
FRED:

MUDDLES: To put up a picture I hammer'd a nail,
                        And the wall fell down with an ear-splitting crash!

NURSE: And the water flow'd in with a splish, splosh,
                                                        splash!

HERBERT: And blew the main fuse in a blinding flash!

MUDDLES, NURSE,   If you want a good job done badly -
& HERBERT: Do it yourself.

FRED: If you want a good job done badly, etc.

                        I tried my hand at the carpentry lark
                        And just gave my thumb a most terrible bash!

MUDDLES: And the wall fell down with an ear-splitting crash!

NURSE: And the water flow'd in with a splish, splosh,
                                                        splash!

HERBERT: And blew the main fuse in a blinding flash!

ALL: If you want a good job done badly -
                            Do it yourself!

                        If you want a good job done badly,
                            Do it yourself, says us,
                        Save up some dough, and have a go,
                            And soon you will start to cuss.

ALL: (continued - getting faster and faster)
                    For look at the dangers of "Do-it-yourself"
                    All you achieve is a horrible hash,
                    He /I just gave his /my thumb a most terrible bash!
                    And the wall fell down with an ear-splitting crash!
                    And the water flow'd in with a splish, splosh,
                                                        splash!
                    And blew the main fuse in a blinding flash!
                    If you want a good job done badly -
                       Do it yourself!

(All exit R. Enter BARON L.)

BARON: When are those confounded Robbers going to report to me?

ROBBERS: (jumping on from R.) Now!

BARON: Aah! Don't do that. Well, what news?

HERBERT: The deed is done.

BARON: Splendid! How did you do it?

ROBBERS: We - er ...

HERBERT: Shot 'em.   } (Together)
FRED: Poisoned 'em.

(BARON looks at them and they exchange nervous glances)

ROBBERS: No, we - we ...

HERBERT: Strangled 'em.   } (Together)
FRED: Suffocated 'em.

BOTH: Stabbed 'em! (they shake hands in self-congratulation)

BARON: Well, which was it?

HERBERT: All of 'em. We wanted to make a really good job of it.

BARON: And you're sure they're quite, quite dead?

HERBERT: Absolutely. (folds his arms)

FRED: Positively. (folds his arms)

ROBBERS: Irrefutably. (they cross their feet) You'll never see
       them alive again.

(POLLY runs on L.)

POLLY: Baron, they're back!

HERBERT: Scarper!

(ROBBERS move to R. door)

BARON: Who's back?

(MARION runs on through R. door)

MARION: Baron, they're here!

(ROBBERS get down on their knees and crawl in front of BARON to L)

BARON: Who's here?

(MUDDLES runs on through L. door)

MUDDLES: Baron, they're safe!

(ROBBERS turn and crawl back to R)

BARON: Who's safe?

(NURSE runs on through R. door)

NURSE: The Babes! The Babes!

(ROBBERS turn and crawl back to L)

BARON: What do you mean?

(WUFFLES runs in through L. door barking joyfully. ROBBERS give up and sit despondently on their haunches)

BARON: (to WUFFLES) And a fat lot of help you are. What are you all babbling about?

NURSE, MARION,
POLLY &   The Babes are home again!
MUDDLES:

WUFFLES: (nodding affirmatively) Wuff-wuff.

BARON: Home again? How can they be? They're dead.

(BABES, followed by ROBIN run on R)

BABES: No, we're not!

BARON: Curses!

ROBIN: Though it's little thanks to you they aren't.

BARON: (rounding on ROBBERS) You fibbers! You bunglers!
You - you -

SUSAN: Uncle, you mustn't be beastly to them. Fred's nerves won't stand it.

ROBIN: I think you have some explaining to do, Baron.

BARON: All right, I admit it. I tried to have them killed.

NURSE, MARION,
POLLY &   You?
MUDDLES:

NURSE: You naughty man. I've a good mind to put you across my knee and spank you. Say you're sorry to Sammy and Susie at once.

BARON: I'm sorry, children.

SUSAN: That's all right, uncle.

SAMMY: It was rather fun, really.

BARON: Now I suppose you'll go and report me to the Sheriff.

MARION: But you are the Sheriff.

BARON: No, they found out I was embezzling the taxes and kicked me out. (rubbing behind) Literally.

BABES: Oh, poor Baron.

BARON: No, I'm not even a Baron any more. I've been outlawed. (to ROBIN) I say, any vacancies in your lot? Oh no, you're not an outlaw any more, are you?

ROBIN: What do you mean?

BARON: Oh, of course, the news came while you were searching for the Babes. King Richard has returned from the Crusades and sent a free pardon to you and all your men and restored to you your title and your lands.

MARION: Robin, how wonderful!

ROBIN: Yes, now I can honourably ask for your hand in marriage Baron, as Maid Marion's guardian, will you -

BARON: Yes, yes - anything to oblige.

POLLY: Muddles and I want to get married too.

MUDDLES: Do we? Oh yes, I suppose we do.

BARON: Anybody else?

NURSE: Yes, me.

BARON: Who to?

NURSE: You, so I can keep an eye on you. And I tell you what, we'll adopt the Babes. Being a father will keep you out of mischief.

BABES: Oh, yes!

ROBBERS: What about us?

SUSAN: You'll have to come and live with us. I don't want Fred to go off and marry someone else before I'm old enough.

WUFFLES: (sits up begging) Wuff-wuff?

ROBIN: You, Wuffles? You shall have three bones a day for the rest of your life.

WUFFLES: (delighted) Wuff!

SUSAN: So now we can all live happily ever after.

ALL: Hurray!

  MUSIC 58. Reprise 21 "A HAPPY SONG"

BLACKOUT

(Close traverse tabs)

Scene Thirteen. GOOD AND BAD

(Tabs)

(MUSIC 59. Enter DEMON L.)

DEMON: This happiness puts me to shame.
Alas! where is my once great fame?
Did'st ever see a sorrier sight
Than Demon stripp'd of all his might?

(He cries quietly. MUSIC 60. Enter FAIRY R.)

FAIRY: How now, Demon? Why, what's awry?
I never thought to see thee cry.

DEMON: I never thought to see myself
Defeated by a pesky elf.
But so it is and being so,
At least leave me alone with woe.
Soon you'll have time enough to weep
When I do die and evil sleep.

FAIRY: How should that give me cause to pine?

DEMON: Because thy work relies on mine.
Thy talents will soon rusty grow.

FAIRY: From lack of use?

DEMON: Exactly so.

FAIRY: Why then, I see the answer plain -
I shall let thee go free again.

DEMON: Aha!

FAIRY: But only for a time;
Just once a year for pantomime.

DEMON: So be it; I'm no longer sad,
Good is no use without some bad.

FAIRY: No, no, thou hast not understood -
Bad is no use without some good.

MUSIC 61. "A LITTLE BIT OF ..."

(Words and Music by John Crocker, arr., Eric Gilder)

DEMON: A little bit of evil -

FAIRY: But not too much.

DEMON: A tiny dash of wickedness -

FAIRY: Just a touch.

DEMON: For good to flourish there must be some bad,
Without 'twould perish which would be very sad.

FAIRY: A little bit of goodness -

DEMON: But not a lot.

FAIRY: A tiny dash of saintliness -

DEMON: Just a jot.

FAIRY: For bad to flourish there must be some good,
                          Without 'twould perish and I don't think it should.

    (Dance)

BOTH: Since one without the other is null and void,
                          We must stick together or be unemploy'd.
                          For each to flourish there must be a pair,
                          An arrangement which strikes us as very fair.

    (Open traverse tabs. MUSIC 62.)

Scene Fourteen. THE EARL OF
HUNTINGDON'S WEDDING RECEPTION

(Fullset. A palace scene. Cut-out ground-row balustrade along back of rostrum. Steps down in C. of rostrum. Palace wings L. and R)

(CHORUS enter from R. & L. on rostrum in pairs. Each pair meets in C. of rostrum and comes D. C. to take their bow. They then split and back away to form diagonal lines R. & L. The principals follow a similar procedure, forming diagonal lines in front of CHORUS. FAIRY from R., backing R., & DEMON from L., backing L: WUFFLES from R., backing R: BARON from L., backing L: HERBERT from R. and FRED from L., both backing R: POLLY from L., backing R: MUDDLES from R., backing R: NURSE from L., backing L: SUSAN from R. and SAMMY from L., both backing L: ALL turn in as MARION enters from R. and ROBIN from L. and meet in C. of rostrum. MUSIC 63. Fanfare.)

ALL: Hurray!

(ROBIN and MARION move down to take their bow. Principals move down into straight line with them. CHORUS move up onto rostrum.

ROBIN: And thus, good friends, our tale is done.

MARION: I have a handsome husband won.

POLLY: And me.

NURSE: Me too - well, could be worse.

SUSAN: And now, as we've been taught by Nurse -

SAMMY: Always to try to be polite,

BOTH: We wish you one and all -

ALL: Goodnight!

(MUSIC 64. FINALE)

                  And now the time has gone; our tale is done,
                  And so we hope that you have all had fun,
                     And fondly wish you as you go along,
                     That you sing a HAPPY SONG.

CURTAIN

PROPERTY AND FURNITURE PLOT

PART ONE

Scene One

OFF L.

2 scrolls	BARON
Business card	DEMON
Prop car	ROBBERS

(Cut-out mounted on shallow frame running
on four trolley wheels.
Cut-out should be made sufficiently high so
that when standing behind it ROBBERS look
as if seated. This will enable them to be
concealed from view if they crawl behind it
on their first entrance. There is a hinged
bonnet flap on front of car, a small practical
driver's door and a notice:- "DIRTY DEEDS
UNLIMITED CO., PROPS., HORRIBLE
HERBERT, (WORMWOOD SCRUBS,
PENTONVILLE). FRIGHTFUL FRED,
(BORSTAL FAILED). ROBBERS OF THE
FINEST HOUSES IN ENGLAND").

List	FRED
Tin Sheriff's star	BARON

OFF R.

Steering wheel and column with bulb horn. A letter.	MUDDLES
Square breakable horseshoe. A nail.	POLLY
Pram with shafts attached.	NURSE & WUFFLES
Reins	WUFFLES
Stick with bone dangling on string.	NURSE
Catapult and paper pellet	SAMMY
Bag of gold	ROBIN

To be thrown on:-

    Prop horseshoe

    Prop sledgehammer

    Prop anvil

PERSONAL

FAIRY	Wand
BARON	Handkerchief

CHORUS	Pound note each
ROBIN	Horn
HERBERT	Pair of pistols, sword, dagger
FRED	Popgun, sword, dagger, notebook and pencil

Scene Two

OFF L.

Schoolbooks	BABES
Nurse's schoolbooks	WUFFLES
Catapult and paper pellet	NURSE
Children's slates with slate pencils attached	CHORUS

Scene Three

SET ON STAGE:- 2 benches diagonally L.

2 benches diagonally R.

Blackboard on easel U.L.C.

Desk U.R.C., with cane, chalk and duster on it, and papers and music sheets under flap of desk

Chair behind desk

School bell

OFF R.

Slates and slate pencils	BABES
Newspaper. Slate and slate pencil	BARON
Small Union Jack. Slate and slate pencil	MUDDLES
Slate and slate pencil	POLLY
Book	1st CHORUS
Slates and slate pencils	ROBBERS

Scene Four

OFF R.

| Lollipop | FRED |

Scene Five

SET ON STAGE:- Double bed L.C. Towel on end of it

Chair to L. of double bed, with pair of socks, one with large hole in heel and needle and darning wool

Single bed R.C. Towel on end of it. Nightgown, mobcap and bedsocks set at head

Table between beds with very large Castor Oil bottle, vast spoon and bag of sweets

Waterproof cloth D.S. of beds in C.

OFF R.

Candle in candlestick	HERBERT
Matchbox	FRED
Large tin bath with 2 bars soap, 2 scrubbing brushes, 2 mops and a washboard	NURSE and MUDDLES
Candle in candlestick	SAMMY
4 buckets water	NURSE and MUDDLES
Kennel with "WUFFLES" over opening. Large hot water bottle and small lampost set inside kennel	WUFFLES

PART TWO

Scene Eight

OFF R.

Staff	MUDDLES
Stand with arrows and 2 bows (one trick bow made with hinge inside and small flat cupboard· bolt on outside)	MUDDLES
Stretcher and boxing gloves	CHORUS
2 bags of gold	BARON
Bow	ROBIN

CHECK - Horn, ROBIN.

OFF L.

Large watch, (Face has only "THEY'RE OPEN!" where 12 would be and "THEY'RE SHUT" where 6 would be, with single hand)	WUFFLES
Bar of chocolate	FRED
Catapult and conker (made of sponge rubber)	SAMMY
Babes' clothes	HERBERT
Arrow, to be attached to her behind	NURSE
Target with arrow in middle	CHORUS
Bows and arrows	CHORUS

TO BE BROUGHT THROUGH AUDITORIUM

Pair of boxing gloves. Bundle of music	POLLY

Scene Ten

SET ON STAGE:- Leaves on either side of ramp

OFF R.

Leash	WUFFLES
Large curved pipe. Large magnifying glass	MUDDLES
Conker. String. Handkerchief	SAMMY

Scene Eleven

OFF L.

Large black chest marked "SAMMY AND SUSAN".
In chest, a paper. Hammer and chisel.　　　　　　BARON

　　　　　　CHECK - Handkerchief, BARON

Scene Twelve

SET ON STAGE:- Large trestle table C., with rolls of wallpaper
　　　　　　and a toilet roll on it.
　　　　　　Under table: 2 buckets, 2 mops, 2 hammers, nails.

　　　　　　U.L., a stepladder

　　　　　　U.R., a stepladder, without stretch ropes

OFF L.

Small pot of Gripfix with tiny brush　　　　　　MUDDLES

EFFECTS PLOT
PART ONE

Scene One

1	Crash of falling metal	Off R.
2	Glass crash, (bucket of broken glass thrown into second bucket)	Off R.
3	Horn sound	Off R.
4	Horn sounded nearer	Off R.
5	Motor car engine	Grams or Tape

Scene Five

6	Thunder, (thunder sheet)	Off, as convenient
7	Thunder	" " "
8	Clatterings and bangings	Off R.

Scene Eight

9	Loud crash	Off L.
10	Ping of bow, (plucked string instrument)	Off. R.

<u>Scene Ten</u>

| 11 | Wind noise, (wind machine) | Off, as convenient |

<u>Scene Eleven</u>

| 12 | Glass crash | Off L. |

MUSIC PLOT
PART ONE

1   Overture

<u>Scene One</u>

2	Opening Chorus, "MERRYDOWNDERRY"	Chorus
3	Baron's entrance music	Orch.
4	Maid Marion's entrance music	"
5	"MY MAN"	Marion and Chorus
6	Muddles' entrance music	Orch.
7	Polly's " "	"
8	"A WONDERFUL LESSON"	Polly and Muddles
9	Fairy's music	Orch.
10	Demon's "	"
11	" ", reprise 10.	"
12	Babes' entrance music	"
13	Nurse's " ", reprise 12	"
14	"A ROOF TO HIS HEAD"	Nurse and Babes
15	Robin's entrance music	Orch.
16	"THE SPICE OF LIFE"	Robin and Chorus
17	Robbers' music	Orch.
18	" ", reprise 17	"
19	" " " "	"
20	"DANGER OF LOVE"	Robin and Marion
21	"A HAPPY SONG" (continue, orchestra only, as link to next scene)	Ensemble

Scene Two

22	Robbers' music, reprise 17	Orch.
23	"YOU GOTTA HAVE BRAINS"	Robbers
24	"OFF TO SCHOOL", reprise 2	Chorus

Scene Three

25	"LITTLE POLLY FLINDERS" (Continue, orchestra only, as link to next scene)	Ensemble

Scene Four

26	Wuffles' music	Orch.
27	Robbers' " , reprise 17	"
28	"JOUST A MOMENT", (Continue, orchestra only, as link to next scene)	Robin, Marion and Babes

Scene Five

29	Robbers' music, reprise 17	Orch.
30	"MANY YEARS AGO"	Nurse
31	Robbers' music, reprise 17	Orch.
32	Scene Finale, (Continue, orchestra only, as link to next scene)	Robin

Scene Six

33	Demon's music, reprise 10	Orch.
34	Fairy's " " 9	"
35	Fairy's beckoning music	"

Scene Seven

36	Ballet	Fairy, Chorus, Demon, Babes & Robbers
37	Entr'acte	

PART TWO

Scene Eight

38	"FUN OF THE FAIR"	Marion and Chorus
39	"OLDE ENGLISHE DANCE"	Ensemble
40	Robbers' music, reprise 17	Orch.
41	Wuffles' " " 26	"
42	Reprise 32, (Continue, orchestra only, as link to next scene)	Robin

Scene Nine

| 43 | "BOW-WOW!" (Continue, orchestra only, as link to next scene) | Nurse and Audience |

Scene Ten

44	"THE SPICE OF LIFE", reprise 16	Robin and Chorus
45	Robbers' music, reprise 17	Orch.
46	Fight music	"
47	Demon's music, reprise 10	"
48	" " " "	"
49	Fairy's " " 9	"
50	Bird Ballet	Fairy and Chorus
51	Reprise 35	Orch.
52	"Greensleeves" (Continue as link to next scene)	"

Scene Eleven

| 53 | Baron's music, reprise 3 | Orch. |
| 54 | "MEN!" (Continue, orchestra only, as link to next scene) | Marion and Polly |

Scene Twelve

55	Robbers' music, reprise 17	Orch.
56	" " " "	"
57	"DO IT YOURSELF"	Nurse, Muddles and Robbers
58	"A HAPPY SONG", reprise 21 (Continue, orchestra only, as link to next scene)	Ensemble

Scene Thirteen

59	Demon's music, reprise 10	Orch.
60	Fairy's " " 9	"
61	"A LITTLE BIT OF ..."	Demon and Fairy
62	"A HAPPY SONG", reprise 21 (for link and continuing as walk-down accompaniment)	Orch.

Scene Fourteen

| 63 | Fanfare | Orch. |
| 64 | Finale, reprise 21 | Tutti. |